The
HOME AND
HAPPINESS
Botanical Handbook

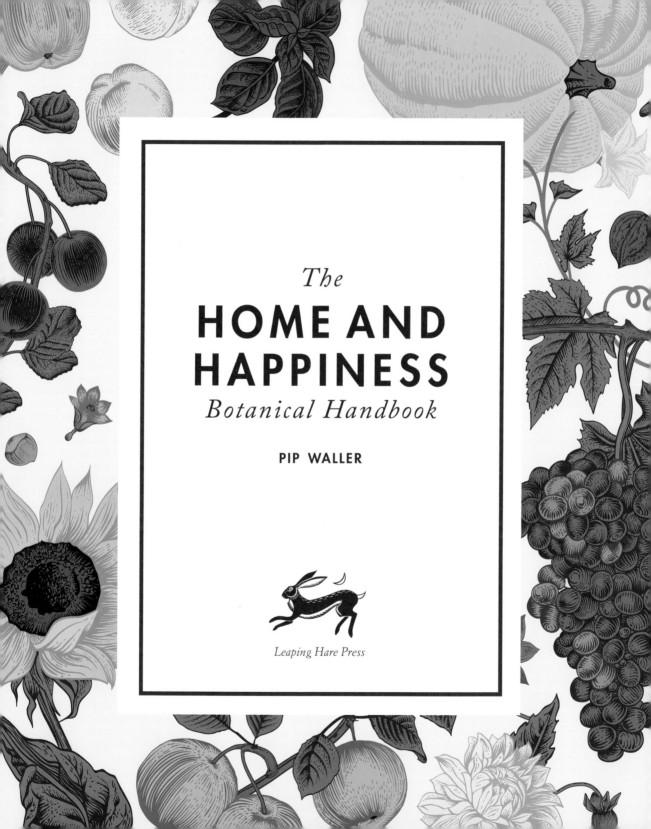

The
HOME AND HAPPINESS
Botanical Handbook

PIP WALLER

Leaping Hare Press

This book is for God as S/He is expressed as the myriad variety and beauty of the plant kingdom,
and for all those who love our beautiful planet.

First published in the UK in 2021 by
Leaping Hare Press

An imprint of The Quarto Group
The Old Brewery, 6 Blundell Street
London N7 9BH, United Kingdom
T (0)20 7700 6700
www.QuartoKnows.com

Some recipes in this book were first published in *The Domestic Alchemist* (2015)

Text copyright © 2015, 2021 Pip Waller
Design and layout copyright © 2017, 2021 Quarto Publishing plc

British Library Cataloguing-in-Publication Data
A catalogue record for this book is available from the British Library

ISBN: 978-0-7112-5671-2
Ebook ISBN: 978-0-7112-5672-9

This book was conceived, designed and produced by
Leaping Hare Press

58 West Street, Brighton BN1 2RA, UK

Publisher David Breuer
Editorial Director Tom Kitch
Art Director James Lawrence
Commissioning Editor Monica Perdoni
Design Manager Anna Stevens
Designer Wayne Blades
Publishing Assistant Chloe Murphy

Printed in China

2 4 6 8 10 9 7 5 3 1

While the publisher and author have made every effort to ensure that the information
contained in this book is accurate and presented in good faith, no warranty is provided
nor results guaranteed. The publishers and author exclude liability to the fullest extent
of the law for any consequence resulting from reliance upon the information contained
herein. Readers should always consult a qualified medical practitioner or therapist before
undertaking a new diet or health programme.

CONTENTS

Chapter One

THE PLANT REVOLUTION

THERE IS A GREEN REVOLUTION happening all around us, with people everywhere turning to plants in search of more natural ways to care for their home and garden. Throughout history and across cultures, plants have been used for food, shelter, clothes, hygiene and medicine, among other things. Plants contain the proteins and other nutrients that all animals need to thrive, so we depend on them for our survival. The soil itself is nourished by living plants, and even when they die, they decompose to form soil from which new plants can grow. Plants sustain all life; everything we need can be obtained from plants.

Today, however, the central role plants play in human lives has been almost forgotten in the Western world. After several generations of urbanized living, those in modern industrialized countries are far removed from nature and rely on polluting man-made chemical products, many of which damage the living world we depend on. And among those of us who live in rural areas, many no longer regularly cultivate, gather and use the helpful plants that grow all around us.

We have become reliant on harsh, often toxic and highly polluting man-made products to care for our bodies, ourselves, our homes and our gardens. These not only damage our own health, but that of our planet. The average household cleaning or laundry product comes with health warnings – if you start to look at packets, you will see alerts such as 'Contains VOCs' (volatile organic compounds), which hurt the lungs and contribute to respiratory disease, and 'Dangerous to aquatic life', which speaks for itself. Then there is the increasing level of plastic waste,

in our landfills and oceans, now such a serious problem that everyone is aware of it (not just dedicated environmentalists).

Fortunately, the plant world holds many solutions, and the individual contributions we can each make will combine to form an avalanche of positive change. The previous volume in this series, *The Health and Beauty Botanical Handbook*, covered the use of plants in caring for the body. This book details what the natural world can offer in caring for our homes and gardens.

NATURAL CLEANING

Natural methods of cleaning are not new.
Previous generations knew all about them:
how to use plants high in natural saponins for
their detergent properties; how to make soap
from mixing alkaline lye (from wood ash) with
oils from plants; how to make and use vinegar
to cut through grease; how certain plants kill
microbes and deter insects; how to use kitchen
staples such as bicarbonate of soda and lemon as
powerful cleaning agents; how to beautify the
home with paints made from flour, plant oil and
other natural pigments; how to colour fabrics
using natural plant dyes; how to protect the
home and create the desired atmosphere using
ancient knowledge about the energetic properties
of herbs. This book contains all this and more.

MODERN PROBLEMS,
OLD-FASHIONED SOLUTIONS

We are living in extraordinary times, when the
plight of our planet is almost daily front-page
news. Plastics fill the oceans, there are concerns
about carbon footprints, and increasing
allergies linked to overuse of strong disinfectant
and endocrine-disrupting chemicals (EDCs as
the World Health Organization calls them) are
implicated in many serious and life-threatening
diseases. These EDCs are found in an alarming
array of household products, including cleaning
sprays, washing and laundry products, paints,
dyes in clothes and furniture, flame retardants
and more – not to mention in plastics that then
leach into our food and drink.

It can be very disturbing to learn about
the seriousness of the situation, but a great
antidote to a problem is the finding of solutions.
Fortunately, the natural world offers countless,
ecologically sound and healthy alternatives for
the needs of the modern household. This book
details over 175 of these, and hopefully will
encourage the reader to start their own lifelong
journey of discovery into the abundant help on
offer from the plant world.

IMPROVING YOUR WELL-BEING
WHILE HELPING THE PLANET

Making your own plant-based products for
the home and garden provides many sources
of satisfaction. Being outside in nature gathering
plants or tending pot herbs on your windowsill,
drying and preparing those you have grown,
and measuring out dried herbs and oils bought
in for making products are all wonderful
activities that connect us to nature, bringing
increased harmony and balance into our lives.
Pottering around in your kitchen laboratory
is great fun. You will embark on an empowering
journey of exploration as you discover how
easy it is to make your own cleaning and other
household products super-charged with the
power of herbs and plant oils. Knowing that you

are part of the great movement to save the planet by reducing the amount of toxins and waste your home contributes, you will love using your plant-based, low- or zero-waste natural home-care products.

In short, plants contribute to our happiness and well-being in so many different ways. Their inherent usefulness isn't the only joy they bring.

CONNECTING WITH THE NATURAL WORLD

This is a book for anyone with an interest in using plants in the home. Whether an expert in the field or a complete novice, you will find recipes to use as they are, or to adapt as you gain confidence. It's a book for you if you're looking to live a more natural life, to reduce your reliance on polluting man-made chemicals, to move towards becoming 'zero waste' in your home and to connect with the natural world – whether you live in a semi-rural location (as I do) or a block of flats in a city.

The recipes in this book include offerings to use all over your home and garden, from laundry detergent to air freshener, from wall paint to garden sprays. Some are simple, requiring almost no equipment; others are complex, such as making soap or your own white vinegar from scratch. My hope is that as your confidence grows, you will begin to experiment and create your own variations. The next few pages are dedicated to showing you all that you need to start your plant-based preparations at home. They include equipment, key ingredients traditionally used in natural cleaning products, basic information on sourcing and storing plants and some key techniques for preservation.

I hope this book helps to lead you on a rich journey of discovery.

Chapter Two

SOURCING HERBS

SOURCING HERBS NEEDS a little thought. Whether you choose to pick herbs in the wild, grow your own or buy them, you will need a certain amount of background knowledge. The following pages are dedicated to providing a few guidelines, and you can also use the Herb Directory on pages 118–37 as a starting point to help identify and source plants.

You will need to purchase some key ingredients such as bicarbonate of soda and vegetable oil that are used in soap making and other recipes. However, even if you begin by buying all of your ingredients, I hope that as your confidence grows you will be inspired to take a step further and discover living plants in nature. The feeling of connection that a human can have with the plant world is irreplaceable in its health-giving and balancing propensity. When you get to know living plants, you will begin to see friends everywhere you go.

IN THE WILD

Foraging, or wildcrafting, is increasingly popular, and you need not live in the woods to do it. It's amazing how many useful herbs grow in the nooks and crannies of a city. However, when gathering from the wild there are a few important considerations.

Always treat the environment with respect and don't over-forage. A good guideline is to always take a little under half of what is there – and if the plant is endangered, don't take any at all. If you are gathering the root of a plant, or a whole plant (as opposed to just some flowers, leaves, stems or bark), then plant some seeds or a new plant. With some plants, you can divide the roots and replant half again.

It's also important to ensure that you are not trespassing on private land, and to check local regulations about gathering plants.

Plant identification is an invaluable skill, and there are excellent books with clear photographs to help the lone learner. If you take this route, you must be extremely careful not to use the wrong plant: if you're not sure, leave it alone. Although this book does not contain recipes for internal use, and while few plants are seriously poisonous, some can harm you even if used by mistake. There are useful resources online about foraging, and I have included some at the back of this book.

Before I pick, I follow the native tradition of asking the plant's permission in my heart (respecting a 'no' if I feel I hear one), and offering gratitude and something in return. In Europe, the traditional offering is oats or barley; in North America, it is tobacco. Even if this seems strange to you, I encourage you to try it. You may be surprised at the warmth it brings you. The earth is a living treasury, and the more you recognize its offerings, the richer your life will be.

GROWING HERBS

Plants are in general easy to please. They like enough (but not too much) light, water and food, and the right kind of soil. They also respond to love: talking to your plants and caring for them actually makes them grow more abundantly. This attitude can be even more important than the quality of the earth in which they are grown,

as shown by the famous eco-community of Findhorn, near Forres in Scotland, who have grown impossibly enormous vegetables on soil that was little more than dirt-covered rock.

You can grow a few herbs anywhere. They are ideal for urban settings and don't require a lot of space. Many will thrive in a windowbox or containers as well as planted in the ground. Lots of herbs – 'herbs' being the general word for describing plants used in medicine, or to give flavour and texture in cooking – are especially easy to grow. Many well-known aromatic culinary herbs are high in antimicrobial properties that are often used in cleaning preparations. Most plants love some attention. The more you pick the flowers of the marigold, for example, the more it will flower. And most plants prefer a sheltered spot and the company of other plants. Check for any individual requirements of the herbs you grow, and grow them simply, using organic or bio methods for maximum benefit.

Start growing whatever you feel like and whatever you can easily find. You can sow seeds – try marigold (*Calendula officinalis*) as an easy starter. Or buy small plants to start you off such as oregano, marjoram or thyme. Make inquiries locally to see what grows well in your area, and just try growing it. Make friends with local gardeners – they will give you tips and maybe also some plants to start you off. You might even find a local allotment to get involved with. Try planting things inside or outdoors. If they are happy, continue as you are; if not, try something else. It is likely you will be pleasantly occupied and satisfied with your home-grown results.

PICKING HERBS

Harvest plants on a sunny day, picking leaves and flowers around mid-morning when the dew has dried. Remember to take a small penknife. Keep an eye on the plants you want so that you can pick them at their peak. Choose the healthiest plants or parts of plants. If you plan to use them fresh in a recipe, try to pick and use immediately.

DRYING & STORING HERBS & PLANTS

Wash plants, if necessary, then remove and compost unhealthy or unnecessary parts. Gather the aerial parts (those above ground) into a bundle and tie up at the bottom of the stalks, or put them into a paper bag. Hang the bundle or bag in a warm, well-ventilated place, indoors or outside. Herbs take up to several days to dry depending on the conditions.

All parts of the plant can be spread out in a single layer on trays to dry in a warm, well-ventilated place. Use mesh trays or trays lined with clean dish towels or paper. Turn the plant matter daily to encourage even drying. Roots can be left whole or roughly chopped (it's easier to cut them fresh). Flowers and leaves are easier to remove from stems when dry. You can also dry plant material in a dehumidifier.

Aim to dry the plant material enough to stop it turning mouldy, without taking all the life away. Store your dried plants in paper bags sealed from the air, or in airtight jars, and keep away from direct sunlight. If dried well, herbs will keep with full properties for at least a year.

BUYING HERBS & OTHER SUPPLIES

Our climate is not suitable for growing all the herbs you may want to use, while growing or foraging your own may not be a suitable choice for you. Whatever the case, what cannot be grown or foraged can be bought. Choose organically grown ingredients as much as possible. Be responsible when buying foraged herbs, and ensure they were properly picked with sustainability in mind. Reputable suppliers of herbs can be found easily online, and you may be lucky and have a good herbal shop near enough to visit. Find a local herbal practitioner and ask his or her advice about local suppliers. This could also put you in touch with a qualified professional, who you could consult about health issues when you need to.

When you are buying herbs in a relatively raw state – for example, dried to use in a recipe – you will easily be able to tell the quality by looking, smelling and tasting a little.

In addition, many of the recipes in this book include ingredients you will need to buy, such as essential oils and plant oils. All of these are available online or from health-food shops.

Chapter Three

KITCHEN SET-UP

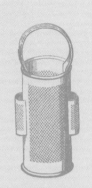

MUCH OF THE EQUIPMENT and key ingredients you will need to start creating useful eco, plant-based preparations and household products you will already have at home, but you should prepare your working area and acquire a few necessary items before you get started. The basic kit on page 21 lists essential pieces of equipment and explains how to use them. The recipes in this book assume you have this kit, and the base ingredients, so they will note only additional 'specialist' items not included in this section.

Before you move on to the recipe section, you will need some knowledge of the basic methods used in home cleaning, and some of the key techniques for preserving and extracting the active ingredients of plants. The following pages are dedicated to this, and you will be referred back to this section frequently during the course of the book.

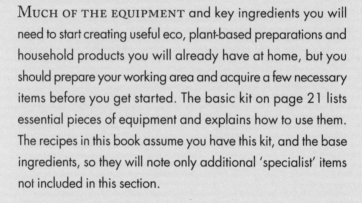

KEY INGREDIENTS

There are some key ingredients that form the basis of many of the recipes in this book. As our grandmothers knew, a lot can be done with a few basics. These include detergents (soap), organic acids such as vinegar and citric acid (from lemon juice for instance), and alkalines such as ordinary bicarbonate of soda and its relation, washing soda. Strong alcohol also acts as a useful cleanser.

Water

The original and often best cleansing substance has to be water. But will any old water do? The answer is complicated! When making any preparation you should use only good-quality water. Unless you have access to pure spring water, filtered water is best, being both cleaner than average tap water and more eco-friendly than bottled water.

Water contains variable amounts of minerals, and these give it its 'hardness' or 'softness'. Hard water is rich in minerals, often especially calcium. Although this is good for drinking, it has implications for cleaning. It makes more of a build-up in your kettle and iron, and can create deposits on taps and shower fittings. It can also leave watermarks when you use it to clean fabrics on sofas or in carpets. Hard water makes less of a lather with soap. Vinegar is a good antidote for

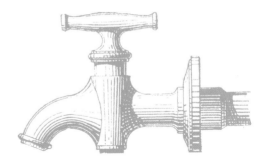

dissolving calcium deposits from hard water as calcium reacts to acids such as vinegar (this is why it's healthy to eat a little vinegar with your green veg – it helps you get the most minerals from them).

Soft water contains fewer minerals and actually feels softer on your skin. It is preferable for cleaning because it doesn't cause soap to scum up or leave mineral stains. On the other hand, soft water lathers much more than hard water, making it more difficult to rinse soap away.

You might have either soft or hard water coming out of your tap at home. If your water is hard, you might want to consider investing in distilled water for making cleaning products. It will be best for certain jobs, especially streak-free cleaning of glass, mirrors and cars, and for stain removal from fabric and upholstery. You can make your own distilled water at home using various methods, including following the advice on how to make aromatic waters, but just using water – no infusion or decoction – in the pressure cooker (p.27).

Soap

Some plants are rich in naturally occurring saponins – soap-like substances that have a cleansing detergent effect. It is relatively simple to make your own natural soap at home from a variety of plant oils mixed with lye. However,

although lye can be made from wood ash, it is generally easier to buy it ready processed. Soap making can seem complex to the beginner, but it really is very doable by following the instructions. This book details two methods: the cold method used to make solid soap bars (which can then be grated to add to powders and other mixtures), and the hot method, which makes an excellent liquid soap. Liquid soap is a vital ingredient for many laundry and home-cleaning products, but if you don't wish to make your own, it is very easy to source and buy.

Vinegar

It is well known that vinegar has a cleaning ability, which is due to its acidity. It is excellent as a cleaner in many circumstances, and can also be used to extract and preserve the useful properties of plants (p.18).

White (clear distilled) vinegar is generally the most used in cleaning products, though you can also use other types. (Cider vinegar is fine for cleaning, but it is not suitable for laundry due to its brown colour.) You will find in these pages a recipe for making your own white vinegar from scratch (p.24). It is also very easily obtainable and can be bought from most supermarkets. Ready-made or home-brewed vinegar is generally 4–7 per cent acetic acid, and it's now also possible to buy very concentrated white vinegar up to 12 per cent. (There is also such a thing as industrial vinegar – 20 per cent acetic acid – which is so strong it requires protective gear to use it.) If you are using any kind of concentrated vinegar, adjust your recipes AND NEVER USE IT IN FOOD. The recipes in this book are written for the ordinary strength stuff (the stuff that can go on your fish and chips no problem).

In some circumstances, you should not use vinegar as it can damage certain surfaces (granite, marble and soapstone surfaces and finished/varnished wood furniture, for instance). This book will give you safe recipes and guidance for when to use which product.

Citric Acid

Citric acid found in lemon juice (and in other plant sources) is another useful acidic cleaning agent. It also has antioxidant and preserving qualities. It is citric acid that gives lemon juice its famous power as a cleaning agent. It is possible to buy pure citric acid powder, which can be made from lemons but is most commonly made from a type of mould. All citrus fruits contain levels of citric acid, and lesser but significant amounts are also present in pineapple, strawberries, raspberries, cranberries, cherries and tomatoes. Citric acid is often used as a preservative and antioxidant in foods, cosmetics and medicines, but it also has a key role to play in natural, non-toxic cleaning products. It is effective at removing coffee and tea stains as well as yellow or brown discolorations (including water and urine stains), and helps remove hard water build-up on dishes and glasses. It is fanastic for cleaning rusted metal and will remove the rust (but always dry metal items after any cleaning as water residues will allow more rust to develop).

Bicarb and Washing Soda

You will have to purchase bicarbonate of soda, which comes from a mineral called trona, found in the beds of ancient dried-up lakes. Much of it comes from Wyoming in the USA, and there is a huge amount of this resource. It provides a powerful alkaline cleansing action that can effectively replace the host of hazardous chemical agents found in modern cleaning products. It is considered to be an excellent eco-friendly option. Washing soda is a close relative of bicarbonate of soda, but slightly stronger. You can buy it, often sold as soda crystals, or make your own by baking your bicarb in the oven.

KEY TECHNIQUES

There are several key methods for extracting the useful properties of plants, which are detailed below. Some recipes in this book will refer you back to this section for instructions.

Herbal Infusions and Decoctions

You can make leaves and flowers as well as ground roots and barks into hot or cold infusions (also called teas or tisanes), steeping either fresh or dried herbs in water. Hot infusions are made by putting dried or fresh herb material into a saucepan with a lid, covering with boiling water and brewing with a lid on the pan for 10–20 minutes. Strain before use. Cold infusions are made by steeping herbs in cold water for 2–3 hours. They are usually made with fresh flowers and leaves.

The parts of a plant that are tougher, such as roots and barks, need to be boiled in water. This is known as a 'decoction', although it can also be called a tea. In making decoctions, the plant matter is put into a saucepan with water, covered with a lid, heated and then simmered for 10–15 minutes. Always make sure you add enough water to allow for evaporation while simmering.

After the infusion or decoction is made, usually (but not always) the liquid is strained off and the solid plant matter is discarded (for composting), although in some cases it can be used – for example, when making soap nut paste (p.29). Straining the liquid through cloth ensures no bits are left – this can be important, for example, to avoid clogging up small tubes in spray bottles.

Infusions and decoctions keep for 3 days in the refrigerator, or longer if citric acid, vinegar and strong alcohol is added to them as part of a cleaning product.

Aromatic Waters

Once you've made an infusion or decoction from an aromatic herb, you can turn it into a 'water', which involves distillation. Some of these are excellent additions to a natural cleaning arsenal, such as witch hazel water and thyme water. A simple method using an adapted pressure cooker – and how to make the two waters mentioned here – is described on page 27. Aromatic waters can keep for anywhere between 3 months and 2 years. If you want to make your own essential oils, start with an aromatic water, from which the essential oil can be separated out.

Herbal Tinctures

Strong alcohol has antimicrobial and cleaning properties and is used in some of the recipes. It is also an excellent extractor and preserver of plant constituents. An alcoholic extract of plants is called a tincture. For any tincture that you might use on or inside the body, only use the best-quality (ideally organic) alcohol. If you are making a tincture as a cleaning product, you can use a clear spirit such as vodka (usually about 40 per cent proof) or the stronger, almost pure alcohol of surgical spirit available in pharmacies. NEVER TAKE SURGICAL SPIRIT INTERNALLY. (Rubbing alcohol, available online, is similar and has the same uses – and the same warnings, which follow below.)

If you are making a tincture with fresh plants, the water in the plants will weaken the proof of the final product. To make a tincture, cover the plant material with between two and five times the amount of alcohol solution in a large jar sealed with a well-fitting lid. For cleaning products it is not vital to be exactly accurate with the amounts – the important thing is that you add enough alcohol to the jar to completely cover the plant material. Leave to sit in a cool, dark place for at least 3 weeks, turning the jar upside down or shaking it roughly once a day.

After 3–8 weeks, strain the liquid through a sieve or funnel lined with muslin. Pull the edges of the cloth up and around the macerated herbs, then twist, wring and press it to extract all of the liquid. Store in a clean bottle. Kept in a cool place away from the sun, a well-made tincture will keep for at least 2 years, some many more.

Strong alcohol like surgical spirit (or rubbing alcohol), and any tincture made from it, is useful as a cleaning and antimicrobial agent. However, there are certain precautions to bear in mind:

- Don't use it on vanished, painted, shellacked or lacquered surfaces as it can damage them.

- It's great on carpets as a stain remover, but never use on delicates or synthetics because it can damage them.

- Never mix with bleach because doing so produces chloroform, which is toxic.

- Never use it anywhere near a spark, flame or fire because it is highly flammable.

- Always use it in a well-ventilated area as it produces vapours that can cause drowsiness or dizziness.

Infused Vinegars

Vinegars are a useful medium for extracting and preserving the herbs used in many home-cleaning products.

Herbal vinegars are made like tinctures. Infuse the herb in 2–3 times the amount of vinegar in a sealed jar, turning daily (if you remember – it will work anyway). Leave to sit for 2–4 weeks in a cool, dark place, then strain through a piece of muslin. You can also use this method to make a lemon-infused vinegar, replacing the herbs with slices of lemon (or other citrus). Vinegars can keep for at least 2 years.

Infused Oils

Vegetable oils can be turned into herbal infused oils, made in the same way as tinctures and vinegars. Infused oils can be used in recipes for polishes, waxes, food wraps and so on.

To make an infused oil, combine 1 part herb with 2–3 parts vegetable oil, then leave to sit for 4–8 weeks in a dark spot to infuse. Once infused, strain and press through muslin, as described for tinctures. You can make an infused oil more quickly by gently heating the herb in the oil, usually in a bain-marie or water bath (p.21), for 2–4 hours.

Vegetable oils often found around the home – linseed, walnut and tung (especially good for wood), as well as olive, sunflower and coconut – are all good choices for making into herbal infused oils. You can use other oils too, depending on what is locally available.

You can use either raw or 'boiled' linseed oil: raw is very slow to dry, so boiled is preferable as it dries more quickly. Ready-prepared boiled linseed oil is nowadays mostly made with toxic additives. However, you can make your own 'boiled' oil by heating raw linseed (flaxseed) oil to 230–238°C (446–460°F). Heat the oil outside on a portable gas ring and never leave it unattended as it can be flammable. Use a probe thermometer and before it reaches 238°C (460°F) maximum, take it off the heat. Homemade boiled linseed oil won't dry as quickly as the chemically treated stuff, but it is completely non-toxic so safe to use around food-preparing surfaces.

Linseed, walnut and tung oils are 'hardening oils', which means they will harden on wood, although they do take a long time to properly dry, longer than chemical-filled modern products. These oils keep well. While olive oil infusions can keep for up to a year before they start to become rancid, and coconut infusions can keep for 2 years, most others will spoil in a few months.

Oils can be made into solid products by the addition of a wax. Traditionally, this was always beeswax. The vegan recipes in this book use carnauba wax instead, which is a much harder, more brittle wax than beeswax, so it is used in smaller quantities.

Essential Oils

Also known as volatile oils, essential oils exist in their pure form in herbs, providing the aroma of any plant. They are extracted from herbs by various methods, the most common being 'steam distillation'. This process is similar to the making of an aromatic water (pp.27–8), only a more concentrated decoction is used to avoid the essential oil being too dissolved in water. The strong aromatic water is then left to stand for some time, usually weeks, in a long tube called a separator. The oil will generally float to the top of the liquid and can then be taken off (what is left at the bottom is a floral or aromatic water).

Soaps

It is easy to make soap, which basically consists of vegetable oils that have been saponified (turned into soap) with a strong alkaloid known as lye. However, soap making involves a lot of steps and some substances that need handling and measuring carefully. For this reason, ingredients for soaps are weighed and you'll need digital scales to make them.

Solid soap is made via a 'cold process' using sodium hydroxide, which involves a lot of stirring and no heat. Liquid soap uses potassium hydroxide in a 'hot process', which involves a lot of stirring and the use of a slow cooker to provide heat. Herbs and essential oils are then added after the oils and lye have been mixed. Soaps keep for years, but they will lose their smell over time as the essential oils evaporate.

LABELLING & STORING

When you have finished making a product, place a label on it that includes the product's name and the date it was made. Most plant-based products should be stored in a cool, dark place in an appropriate vessel. An old cleaning-product bottle simply washed out for re-use will usually suffice, or use an airtight container. This will ensure each product stays at its best for as long as possible. Each recipe includes a recommended shelf life; use this only as a guide, with common sense always prevailing. If a product starts smelling odd, discard it.

HOW TO USE THIS BOOK SUCCESSFULLY

There is a wide range of recipes in this book – from surface cleaners and furniture polish to soaps and air fresheners. To make them successfully, there is some important information you need to keep in mind.

INGREDIENTS

- You will need to purchase several base ingredients for many of the cleaning product recipes: bicarbonate of soda, washing soda, alcohol and essential oils (which you can make yourself but it is a very long and complex process), among others. You may want to buy vinegar or you could brew your own (p.24), and you may wish to make your own liquid soap (p.65) or buy a good-quality liquid Castile soap. In terms of herbs, some recipes are made from fresh, some from dry and others from a mixture. You may need to purchase plants that you can't grow near you, but all the plants used in this book are generally easily available online. Unless fresh or dried herbs are specified, it should be assumed that you can use either for each recipe. If the amounts differ depending on whether you use fresh or dried, this will be stated.

- Some ingredient lists contain premade preparations: tinctures, infused vinegars and so on. Where a specific recipe for these appears in the book, you will be referred to it; otherwise, you will be referred back to the Key Techniques section (pp.17–19) for the standard technique.

EQUIPMENT & METHOD

- Before you start making anything, gather together the basic equipment (p.21). All the recipes assume you have this equipment at hand; only if you need something less common will it be specified.

- Some recipes are simple and others complex. In the interests of space, the various methods are described in full only once, and you will be referred back to them as required. Always carefully read the recipe and the general information found elsewhere in the book, before beginning.

MEASUREMENTS

- Using plants isn't an exact science and many tend to measure by eye to produce the desired result. With this in mind, most recipes use rough approximations. However, some recipes, especially all soaps, require that ingredients be very carefully weighed (because you're using caustic substances and the product won't work if the measurements are wrong).

- In such recipes, tbsp measurements do not provide the necessary accuracy, so they have not been provided and their use is not advised.

- For other recipes, tbsp and tsp measurements provided in this book are based on the following:
  1 tbsp = 15ml
  1 tsp = 5ml
  ½ tsp = 2.5ml

BASIC KIT

Rack, string, paper bags, selection of storage containers, labels

Freshly picked herbs can be tied together and hung from a rack to dry. When dried, store in paper bags or glass jars with tightly fitting lids, away from direct sunlight. Jars are also used to store tinctures, vinegars and infused oils; you may want large ones for this purpose. You will also need old cleaning-product bottles and so forth, plus spray bottles. Almost everything you make will need a label.

Whatever you use to store your preparations needs to be particularly clean. Using dirty bottles and jars for storage means your products won't last as long.

Coffee grinder
For grinding dried herbs and roots and carnauba wax.

Large jars
For making infused vinegars, oils, tinctures, etc. (Old sweet jars are useful if you can get your hands on them.)

Funnels
For pouring and straining. You need both large and small to fit the necks of storage bottles.

Muslin
For straining potions. Use squares of muslin, large cotton handkerchiefs or dish towels.

Sieves and strainers
Metal sieves and strainers, from tea strainer size upwards, are useful for straining. (A small wine press, of the kind normally used for home brewing, is good for pressing out tinctures, infused vinegars, etc.)

Cooking implements
For brewing up mixtures, use pots, saucepans, heat-resistant stainless steel or silicone spatulas and spoons, and a potato masher.

Bain-marie/water bath
For heating potions gently, make a bain-marie by placing a stainless steel bowl over a saucepan of simmering water on the hob or, if you have one, use a stainless steel double boiler. For a water bath, half-fill a flameproof baking dish or saucepan with water on the hob, and place heat-resistant bowls containing your potions inside it.

Measuring equipment
I advise using standard kitchen measuring spoons for all recipes that require tsp or tbsp amounts. Some recipes require accurately weighed ingredients. Digital scales for home use are readily available in kitchen shops, the kitchen section of many department stores and online.

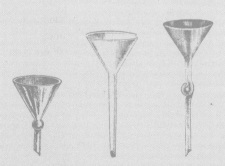

Safety

Surgical spirit is highly flammable and should not be used near sparks or a flame. It should be used in well-ventilated rooms as the vapours can cause drowsiness and dizziness. In addition, it should never be taken internally.

Linseed oil and turpentine are also flammable and should never be left unattended when being heated.

People with delicate, sensitive skin often find borax an irritant, and there is some evidence that it could be harmful to health, especially hormonal health, and the male reproductive system.

Vinegar-based cleaners should not be used on granite, marble and soapstone surfaces and finished or varnished wood furniture.

With any cleaning product, always apply to a small, inconspicuous area of furniture or carpets first before doing the whole thing.

Chapter Four

THE
RECIPES

HOUSEHOLD PRODUCTS

The cleaners in this section are for every surface and room in the house, offering environmentally friendly alternatives to strong-smelling chemicals. The essences and other ingredients leave a fresh scent and are natural disinfectants. The herbs also make perfect room sprays and fragrant potpourri.

White Vinegar

You could purchase 'white' (clear distilled) vinegar from the supermarket, or you can make your own homemade vinegar. Vinegar is made from a mother – a culture of the right kind of bacteria to ferment fruit into alcohol and then vinegar. If you can get 2 litres/3½ pints sugar cane juice, use it in place of water and sugar.

INGREDIENTS
- 2 litres/3½ pints water
- 350g/12½oz sugar
- 5g/⅛oz (1 packet) wine yeast
  (or baking yeast if you can't find wine yeast)
- 500ml/18fl oz raw unfiltered vinegar
  (cider vinegar is fine)

YOU WILL NEED
- A demijohn

MAKES & KEEPS
Makes a variable amount.
Keeps indefinitely if pasteurized.

METHOD
Heat the water and sugar in a large pot to dissolve the sugar. Allow it to cool until it is warm (43.3°C/110°F is the temperature yeast loves best). Pour into a clean demijohn and add the yeast. Put on an airlock and leave at room temperature to ferment (into alcohol) for about 2 weeks or until it stops bubbling.

Next, transfer the liquid to a large glass or ceramic jar with a wide lid, add the raw vinegar and cover with a piece of muslin or other thin cloth to protect from insects while allowing it to breathe. It needs to be stored in a dark area and at room temperature. After a few days, you will see a film beginning to form – this is the vinegar mother. Start tasting it from about 4 weeks to see if it is ready. The first time it can take much longer, up to 2–3 months, as the mother needs to establish. The longer you leave it, the stronger the vinegar gets – and it should be strong for cleaning purposes. When it is ready, pour the vinegar off and strain through a cloth. Once the mother is established, you can use it again to make another batch of vinegar. To do so, carefully remove it and add to your next batch of fermented sugar water, leaving to brew for about a month.

You can pasteurize the vinegar so it will be stable at room temperature. To do this, pour into jars or bottles in a big pot and enough water to cover two thirds of the jars. The lids should be on but loose then bring to the boil and simmer for 1–2 minutes, turn off the heat, leave to cool and tighten the lids.

To make (apple) cider vinegar, follow the instructions above, but add browned apple skins and raw vinegar to the water in place of the sugar.

—Tip—
YOU CAN USE A BALLOON AS A MAKESHIFT AIRLOCK: STRETCH THE BALLOON OVER THE OPENING TO SEAL IT. IF IT INFLATES TOO MUCH AS IT FILLS WITH THE TINY AIR BUBBLES COMING OFF THE FERMENTING LIQUID, LIFT THE SIDE TO RELEASE SOME OF THE AIR.

Chamomile & Marjoram Surface Cleaner

The addition of chamomile and marjoram gives this gentle but effective eco-friendly cleaner a beautiful, sweet scent.

INGREDIENTS

- 500ml/18fl oz White Vinegar (p.24)
- 20g/2 tbsp marjoram flowers and leaves
- 15g/2 tbsp chamomile flower heads
- 20 drops lavender essential oil

MAKES & KEEPS

Makes 500ml/18fl oz. Keeps up to 2 years.

METHOD

Use the vinegar and herbs to make an infused vinegar (p.18). Add the essential oil and decant into a spray bottle (for easy cleaning).

For everyday use, add an equal amount of water to a little of the mixture. Spray on, leave for a few minutes and wipe off.

For really tough jobs, use the cleaner undiluted – gently heating it for a few minutes will make it extra strong. Spray dirty surfaces with the hot vinegar cleaner and leave for 15 minutes before scrubbing and rinsing.

CAUTION

Vinegar based cleaners should not be used on granite, marble and soapstone surfaces and finished/varnished wood furniture.

Lemon Fresh Cleaner

A beautifully simple recipe.

INGREDIENTS

- 500ml/18fl oz White Vinegar (p.24)
- 1 lemon, sliced
- 10 drops lemon essential oil
- 10 drops orange essential oil

MAKES & KEEPS

Makes 500ml/18fl oz. Keeps 1 year or more.

METHOD

Use the vinegar and lemon to make an infused vinegar (p.18), then add the essential oils.

Use in the same way as the Chamomile & Marjoram Surface Cleaner.

All-purpose Cleaning Spray

COURTESY OF MICHAEL VERTOLLI

This cleaner benefits from the addition of liquid soap.

INGREDIENTS

- 200ml/7fl oz water, boiled or distilled
- 50ml/3½ tbsp White Vinegar (p.24)
- 1 drop Castile-style Liquid Soap (p.65)
- 5 drops lavender essential oil
- 3 drops pine essential oil
- 3 drops spruce or fir essential oil
- 1 drop geranium essential oil

MAKES & KEEPS

Makes 250ml/9fl oz. Keeps indefinitely.

METHOD

Combine the ingredients in a spray bottle and shake to mix.

Shake well before use. Spray the surface, then wipe clean.

Bug-busting Surface Cleaner

Thymol in thyme is one of the strongest disinfectants available.

INGREDIENTS

- 500ml/18fl oz White Vinegar (p.24)
- 10-20g/1–2 tbsp thyme leaves
- 10g/2 tbsp marigold petals
- 20 drops thyme essential oil

MAKES & KEEPS

Makes 500ml/18fl oz. Keeps up to 2 years.

METHOD

Use the vinegar, thyme and marigold to make an infused vinegar (p.18), then add the essential oil.

Use in the same way as the Chamomile & Marjoram Surface Cleaner (p.25).

AROMATIC WATERS

Distilling aromatic waters can be a lot of fun – your kitchen will soon resemble an inventor's laboratory. You can either purchase a small copper still or make your own as described here. Aromatic waters have the advantage of having a high volatile oil content so they are antimicrobial and keep for a very long time. They can be made from many plants, and the ones described here are particularly useful as cleaning products. They are ideal for use around babies or anyone extra sensitive to chemicals. Aromatic waters can also be used for food, medicines and skin care.

COURTESY OF JOE NASR

YOU WILL NEED

- A still, or a pressure cooker, 6.3mm (¼in) silicone tubing (from a brewer's shop), hotplate if your cooker is far from your sink

Witch Hazel Aromatic Water

Witch hazel water is very useful as a home-cleaning product: it can be used alone as an antimicrobial surface sanitizer or stain remover, to clean jewellery and as part of other recipes.

INGREDIENTS

- 500g/1lb 2oz fresh witch hazel twigs from flowering branchesor 180g/6oz of dried witch hazel, half each bark and leaves
- 3 litres/5¼ pints water

MAKES & KEEPS

Makes 300ml/10fl oz. Keeps at least 1 year.

METHOD

If you are using fresh witch hazel twigs, strip off the leaves and flowers, and strip the bark from the twigs. Make a decoction (p.17) of the bark, leaves and water by simmering in a pressure cooker on a low heat for 2 hours. Remove from the heat and leave to stand overnight. The next day, put the pressure cooker near the sink (use a hotplate if necessary). Remove the pressure regulator to expose the vent pipe (steam exit). Connect the tubing to the vent pipe. Pass the tubing beneath the water tap and then on and into a 300ml/10fl oz collecting glass bottle. Turn on the heat to high. When the water boils, open the tap to allow cold water to flow around and cool the tubing. Simmer on a low heat. To obtain a good-quality water, the distillation process should be slow with minimum heat; the distillate should not be warm to the touch but cool, ideally 35°C/95°F. Simmer until you have 300ml/10fl oz of distilled witch hazel.

Note: you can also use witch hazel as a simple decoction without distilling it. The decoction will have similar properties but will only keep for up to a week.

—Tip—

YOU CAN POWER UP ANY
SURFACE-CLEANING RECIPE IN
THIS BOOK BY USING WITCH
HAZEL OR THYME AROMATIC
WATER IN PLACE OF WATER.

Thyme Aromatic Water

*This powerful aromatic water is an extremely
strong disinfectant and can be used alone or as a
powerful addition to any antimicrobial cleaner.*

INGREDIENTS
- 150g/5¼oz dried thyme leaves and flowers
  (or 300g/10½oz fresh)
- 2.5 litres/4½ pints water

MAKES & KEEPS
Makes 300ml/10fl oz. Keeps at least 1 year.

METHOD
Put the thyme and water together into a pressure
cooker. Follow the instructions for witch hazel (p.27)
from the point when you attach the tubing to the
vent pipe – no need to decoct the thyme first as it
easily gives up its properties.

Antibacterial Multisurface Cleaner

COURTESY OF TERI EVANS

*This recipe adds the powerful bleach-like effect of borax
to make a strong antibacterial cleaner.*

INGREDIENTS
- 5g/1 tsp borax (see box, p.71)
- 5g/1 tsp bicarbonate of soda
- 10ml/2 tsp lemon juice
- 400ml/14fl oz hot water
- 10 drops tea tree essential oil
- 5 drops eucalyptus essential oil
- 5 drops lavender essential oil

MAKES & KEEPS
Makes about 400ml/14fl oz. Keeps up to 2 months.

METHOD
Put all the ingredients into an empty spray cleaner
bottle. Shake well to mix, repeating vigorously before
each use.

Rinse surfaces after spraying to remove traces of
borax and oils.

Eco-powered Oven Cleaner with Basil

With the addition of a little elbow grease, this is as effective as commercial brands, without the chemicals.

INGREDIENTS

- 120ml/4fl oz Castile-style Liquid Soap (p.65)
- 250g/8¾oz bicarbonate of soda
- 60ml/4 tbsp rosemary vinegar (p.18)
- 4 drops basil essential oil

MAKES & KEEPS

Makes enough for one really thorough clean. Mix the cleaner up freshly each time you need it.

METHOD

Mix all the ingredients thoroughly in a bowl. Remove the oven shelves and clean separately.

Using a paintbrush, spread your mixture over the entire surface of the oven. Leave it for 6–8 hours or overnight. During this time the mixture will foam up slightly and lift the grime from the oven surface.

Using a bowl full of clean water and a damp foam scrubber, wipe out the oven. Change the water as needed. If the oven is really greasy and hasn't been cleaned for a while, repeat the process once more.

Soap Nut Surface Cleaning Paste

A great way to make use of the pulp left over after making soap nut liquid.

INGREDIENTS

- Fruit pulp from boiled soap nuts (p.47)
- 15–30g/1–2 tbsp washing soda
- 10 drops lemon essential oil
- 10 drops thyme essential oil

MAKES & KEEPS

Makes about 4 tbsp. Keeps 2 weeks.

METHOD

Mix the ingredients together and store in a small tub with a lid. To use, apply with a cloth or scouring pad to sinks, baths and other surfaces then rinse.

— Tip —

USE THE ROSEMARY & HORSE
CHESTNUT SCOURING POWDER TO
CLEAN STAINED TEA CUPS – IT'S
QUITE MIRACULOUS.

—Tip—

YOU CAN CROCHET A FABULOUS
BIODEGRADABLE SCOURING PAD
FROM STINGING NETTLE STRING
(P.117), OR FROM GARDEN TWINE.

Rosemary & Horse Chestnut Scouring Powder

Bicarbonate of soda lifts dirt off surfaces and is gently abrasive, so it is ideal for make a scouring powder. Adding dried and ground herbs brings abrasive qualities to the scouring mixture. The conkers from a horse chestnut tree contain saponins, which are soapy.

INGREDIENTS

- 4 dried conkers (the nuts only), ground
- 15g/½oz dried rosemary leaves, ground
- 430g/15⅛oz bicarbonate of soda
- 300g/10½oz gram flour
- 20 drops rosemary essential oil

MAKES & KEEPS

Makes 870g/1lb 14½oz. Keeps 6–12 months.

METHOD

Put all the dry ingredients into a very dry jar (if damp, the bicarbonate of soda will react) with a tight-fitting lid. Shake well to mix. Sprinkle on the essential oil and mix again.

Sprinkle on a damp cloth to clean bath rings, food deposits from the sink, etc. For a cream cleaner, mix a little powder with an equal amount of water to form a paste.

Thyme Disinfectant Scouring Powder

This recipe contains salt, which is abrasive and antibacterial.

INGREDIENTS

- 250g/8¾oz salt
- 15 drops thyme essential oil
- 15g/½oz dried thyme leaves, ground
- 430g/15⅛oz bicarbonate of soda

MAKES & KEEPS

Makes 700g/1lb 8¾oz. Keeps indefinitely.

METHOD

Spread the salt out on a plate and sprinkle thoroughly with the thyme oil. Mix all the ingredients together.

Use in the same way as the Rosemary & Horse Chestnut Scouring Powder.

Ground Coffee Pan Scrub

This simple recipe is both scouring and deodorizing.

INGREDIENTS
- 40g/1⅜oz used ground coffee
- 110g/3⅞oz bicarbonate of soda

MAKES & KEEPS
Makes 150g/5¼oz. Keeps indefinitely.

METHOD
Spread the ground coffee out on a tray somewhere warm to dry. When dry, mix with the bicarbonate of soda, and store in a jar or tub close to the sink.

To use, scoop out some of the mixture and use with a scouring pad to scrub your dirty pans.

—Tip—

YOU CAN ALSO USE THIS POWDER AS A DEODORIZER. SPRINKLE SOME IN THE BOTTOM OF YOUR KITCHEN BIN OR FOOD COMPOSTING BIN, FOR INSTANCE, TO ABSORB BAD SMELLS.

Zesty Washing-up Liquid

Homemade washing-up liquids generally rely on a combination of liquid soap and washing soda for their cleaning power.

INGREDIENTS
- 20g/4 tsp washing soda
- 375ml/13fl oz boiling water
- 75g/5 tbsp Castile-style Liquid Soap (p.65) or ¾ of a 250g/8¾oz bar solid castile soap, grated
- 10 drops lemon or orange essential oil
- 10 drops grapefruit essential oil
- 10 drops tea tree essential oil

MAKES & KEEPS
Makes about 425ml/14½fl oz.
Keeps at least 6 months.

METHOD
If using grated soap, stir into the water until dissolved, then slowly stir in the soda. If not, dissolve the washing soda in the water, then add the liquid soap, continuing to stir until dissolved. Leave to cool. When cool, stir in the essential oils and pour into a bottle.

Shake well before use.

— Tip —

IF YOU USE GRATED SOLID SOAP, YOUR HOMEMADE WASHING-UP LIQUID MAY THICKEN IN THE COLD. USING LESS WASHING SODA WILL GIVE A THINNER LIQUID IF YOU LIVE IN COLDER CLIMES. ALWAYS RINSE WELL AFTER WASHING, AS FOR ANY WASHING-UP LIQUID.

Happy House Washing-up Liquid

This is a variation of the previous recipe, but with the oils used in 'happy house' recipes.

INGREDIENTS

- 20g/4 tsp washing soda
- 375ml/13fl oz boiling water
- 75g/5 tbsp Castile-style Liquid Soap (p.65) or ¾ of a 250g/8¾oz bar solid castile soap, grated
- 15 drops orange essential oil
- 15 drops basil essential oil

MAKES & KEEPS

Makes about 425ml/14½fl oz. Keeps at least 6 months.

METHOD

Make and use in the same way as the Zesty Washing-up Liquid (p.31).

Simple Ivy Washing-up Liquid

This is the simplest plant-powered washing-up liquid. If you can't find ivy, use the same quantity of soapwort instead.

INGREDIENTS

- 2 handfuls/60g/2oz of common ivy leaves (fresh)
- 500ml/18fl oz water
- 10g/2 tsp washing soda

MAKES & KEEPS

Makes 500ml/18fl oz. Keeps 1 week.

METHOD

Put all the ingredients into a saucepan and boil for 5 minutes. Leave to cool. Strain through a cloth into a jar, and it's ready to use.

To use, fill the detergent compartment of the dishwasher, or use directly on dishes to wash, rinsing well afterwards.

Zesty Zero-waste Dishwasher Powder

A citrus-fresh, planet-friendly alternative for using in your dishwasher.

INGREDIENTS

- 280g/10oz salt
- 20 drops lemon essential oil
- 20 drops grapefruit essential oil
- 1.16kg/2lb 9oz washing soda (or half/half borax* and washing soda)
- 250g/8¾oz citric acid

MAKES & KEEPS

Makes 1.7kg/3lb 12oz. Keeps indefinitely.

Spread out the salt in a large dish and sprinkle the essential oils over it. Then put into a large container and shake to mix with the other ingredients. Store in an airtight container.

To use, fill the detergent compartment of the dishwasher. Use with a rinse agent (pp.34–5).

* If using borax, read the caution on page 71.

Sensitive Stomach Dishwasher Powder

This recipe contains oils helpful for a sensitive stomach.

INGREDIENTS

- 280g/10oz salt
- 20 drops chamomile essential oil
- 20 drops lavender essential oil
- 1 kg/2lb 3¼oz washing soda
- 250g/8¾oz citric acid

MAKES & KEEPS

Makes 1.5kg/3lb 5oz. Keeps indefinitely.

Make and use in the same way as the Zesty Zero-waste Dishwasher Powder.

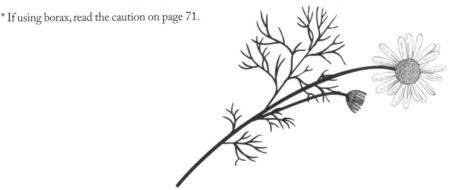

—Tip—

THESE TWO DISHWASHER POWDER RECIPES
CAN BE MADE INTO SMALL TABLETS BY ADDING
A LITTLE WATER AND SQUEEZING THE REQUIRED
AMOUNT INTO A SMALL BALL, LIKE A MINI BATH
BOMB, WITH YOUR HANDS.

Soap Nut Dishwasher Powder

This is a stronger powder with added detergent.

INGREDIENTS
- 215g/7½oz washing soda
- 204g/7¼oz borax (see box, p.71)
- 2 tbsp finely grated Laundry Soap (pp.63–4)
- 2 tbsp finely ground soap nut shells

MAKES & KEEPS
Makes about 440g/15½oz. Keeps 6 months.

METHOD
First read the note on borax on page 71.

Carefully mix everything together in a large container. Store in a jar or box and use in the usual way. (Don't forget to add a rinse agent to the rinse compartment – this is particularly important because the recipe contains soap.)

Dishwasher Rinse Agent

An eco-friendly alternative to ready-prepared rinse aids.

INGREDIENTS
- 2 tbsp citric acid
- 250ml/9fl oz White Vinegar (p.24)
- 10 drops lemon essential oil
- Pinch of turmeric (optional, for colour)

MAKES & KEEPS
Makes 250ml/9fl oz. Keeps indefinitely.

METHOD
Put the citric acid and vinegar into a small saucepan and warm for a few minutes until dissolved. Add the lemon oil and turmeric pour into a storage bottle. Shake before use, then add to the rinse compartment of your dishwasher.

Vinegar-free Dishwasher Rinse Agent

This recipe relies on alcohol instead of vinegar to make your dishes squeaky clean.

INGREDIENTS

- 250ml/9fl oz water
- 80g/3oz citric acid
- ¼ tsp dried turmeric (optional, for colour)
- 500ml/18fl oz vodka
- 15–20 drops lemon essential oil

MAKES & KEEPS

Makes 750ml/1¼ pints. Keeps indefinitely.

METHOD

Mix the water and citric acid in a saucepan and warm for a few minutes until clear. Mix in the turmeric and pour into a bottle. Add the alcohol and lemon oil. Use in the same way as for any other rinse agent.

Rosemary & Pine Toilet Cleaner

Forming the basis of most eco-friendly toilet cleaners, vinegar provides the cleaning power here, and is given a good smell and extra antimicrobial action by the rosemary and pine.

INGREDIENTS

- 500ml/18fl oz White Vinegar or Cider Vinegar (p.24)
- 1 small handful of rosemary leaves
- 1 large handful of pine needles, removed from the stalks
- 50 drops/½ tsp rosemary essential oil (optional)
- 50 drops/½ tsp pine essential oil (optional)

MAKES & KEEPS

Makes about 500ml/18fl oz. Keeps at least 1 year.

METHOD

Use the vinegar and the fresh rosemary and pine needles to make an infused vinegar (p.18). If desired, add the essential oils for a stronger odour.

Pour a bucket of water down the toilet to force water out of the bowl. This will enable you to reach the sides more easily. Then pour the undiluted cleaner into the bowl and leave for 10–20 minutes. Scrub well with a toilet brush.

De-stress Bath-cleaning Bomb

This ingenious recipe actually cleans the tub after your relaxing bath!

INGREDIENTS
- 180g/6⅜oz bicarbonate of soda
- 125g/4⅜oz citric acid
- 120g/4¼oz Epsom salts
- 1–3 tsp water
- 2 tsp lavender essential oil

MAKES & KEEPS
Makes about 450g/1lb. Keeps 6 months.

METHOD
Put the dry ingredients into a large bowl and mix thoroughly using a whisk. Put the water and essential oils into a jar and shake to mix thoroughly. Slowly add the liquid ingredients to the powders in the bowl, whisking gently as you do. When they are all mixed in, pack the mixture into a bath bomb mould, or simply make into roughly 5cm/2in balls with your hands. If the mixture doesn't stick together well, add a tiny bit more water until it does. Let the bath bombs dry out thoroughly (overnight).

To use, add a ball to a running bath. Soak and enjoy. Afterwards, drain the water out and spray the bath lightly with a vinegar-based cleaning spray (pp.25–6) or a shower-fresh spray (opposite) and rinse well to finish the cleaning process started by the bath bomb.

Pain-relief Bath-cleaning Bomb

The perfect bath bomb for aching muscles and joints, this cleans the bath after your pain-relieving soak.

INGREDIENTS
- 180g/6⅜oz bicarbonate of soda
- 125g/4⅜oz citric acid
- 120g/4¼oz Epsom salts
- 1–3 tsp water
- 1 tsp pine essential oil
- 1 tsp rosemary essential oil

MAKES & KEEPS
Makes about 450g/1lb. Keeps 6 months.

METHOD
Make and use in the same way as the De-stress Bath-cleaning Bomb.

Shower-fresh Spray

*A simple way to keep your shower from getting
scummy and greasy.*

INGREDIENTS

- 1 sliced fresh lemon
- 1 handful of fresh thyme/4 tsp dried thyme
- 250ml/9fl oz surgical spirit
- 750ml/1¼ pints water
- 1 tbsp Castile-style Liquid Soap (p.65)
- 20–40 drops lemon essential oil (optional)

MAKES & KEEPS

Makes 1 litre/1¾ pints. Keeps 6 months.

METHOD

Make a tincture (p.17) by covering the lemon
and thyme with the surgical spirit and 250ml/9fl oz
of water. Leave for 2–4 weeks, then strain and
press. Put into a spray bottle, and add the rest of
the ingredients.

To use after each shower, shake before use,
then spray the shower cubicle glass and tiles.
No need to rinse.

Thyme & Marigold Disinfectant

*This powerful disinfectant harnesses the
germ-busting properties of thyme and marigold.*

INGREDIENTS

- 500ml/18fl oz White Vinegar or
  Cider Vinegar (p.24)
- 15g/½ oz dried thyme
  (or 1 handful of freshly picked if possible,
  the leaves removed from the stalks)
- 15g/½ oz dried marigold flowers
  (or 1 handful of fresh)
- 100 drops/1 tsp thyme essential oil

MAKES & KEEPS

Makes about 450ml/16fl oz. Keeps at least 1 year.

METHOD

Use the vinegar, thyme leaves and marigold flowers
to make an infused vinegar (p.18). Add the thyme
essential oil and bottle the mixture.

Dilute with an equal amount of water to wipe down
surfaces, sinks, toilet seats and pet areas.

Minty-fresh Toothbrush Cleaner

For deep cleaning your toothbrush.

INGREDIENTS

- 250ml/9fl oz White Vinegar (p.24)
- 20g/1 handful of fresh mint leaves, finely chopped
- 30 drops peppermint oil

MAKES & KEEPS

Makes about 250ml/9fl oz. Keeps 6 months.

METHOD

Use the vinegar and mint leaves to make an infused vinegar (p.18). When ready, add the peppermint essential oil to the infused vinegar and store in a dark bottle. To use, simply soak your toothbrush in the liquid for 30-60 minutes, then rinse well.

Antibacterial Toothbrush Cleaner

Helps prevent gum disease.

INGREDIENTS

- 250ml/9fl oz White Vinegar (p.24)
- 20g/1 handful of fresh thyme leaves, finely chopped
- 20 drops clove essential oil
- 10 drops thyme essential oil

MAKES & KEEPS

Makes about 250ml/9fl oz. Keeps 6 months.

METHOD

Make and use in the same way as the Minty-fresh Toothbrush Cleaner.

Lemon Zinger Floor Cleaner

Thyme & Marigold Disinfectant forms the base of this floor cleaner, which is ideal for ceramic or vinyl tile floors. Do not use it on a stone floor as the vinegar can erode some types of stone, including marble.

INGREDIENTS
- 250ml/9fl oz Thyme & Marigold Disinfectant (p.37)
- 750ml/1¼ pints White Vinegar (p.24)
- 175ml/6fl oz lemon juice

MAKES & KEEPS
Makes enough for 4 washes. Keeps 3 months.

METHOD
Mix all the ingredients together.

Add 300ml/10fl oz of the floor cleaner to a large bucketful (about 5 litres/8¾ pints) of hot water from the tap. Sweep the floor and clean with a mop (no need to rinse).

Stone Floor Soap

A little linseed in this stone floor cleaner adds extra shine.

INGREDIENTS
- 250ml/9fl oz Castile-style Liquid Soap (p.65)
- 60ml/2 tbsp linseed oil
- 50 drops/½ tsp grapefruit or orange essential oil
- 50 drops/½ tsp tea tree essential oil
- 200ml/7fl oz hot water

MAKES & KEEPS
Makes 450ml/16fl oz. Keeps 3–6 months.

METHOD
Mix the liquid soap together with the linseed oil and essential oils. Pour the hot water over this mixture and stir gently.

To use, add 3 tbsp to a large bucket of very hot water. Sweep the floor and clean with a mop. Rinse with clean water, if desired, but not essential.

Juniper, Rosemary & Lavender Glass Cleaner

This window cleaner contains plants traditionally used for psychic protection.

INGREDIENTS

- 250ml/9fl oz White Vinegar (p.24)
- 25 drops/¼ tsp juniper essential oil
- 25 drops/¼ tsp rosemary essential oil
- 25 drops/¼ tsp lavender essential oil

MAKES & KEEPS

Makes 250ml/9fl oz. Keeps 1–2 years.

METHOD

Put the vinegar and oils into a spray bottle and shake gently. Leave for 24 hours to settle.

To use, add 2 tsp of the cleaner to 1 litre/1¾ pints warm water. Do not use more than this as it will lead to streaks. Apply the diluted cleaner to the glass using a clean cloth or spray from a bottle. Wipe the glass clean with a dry cloth (or old newspaper).

Soap Nut Glass Cleaner

This cleaner is perfect for dirty windows and mirrors.

INGREDIENTS

- 15ml/1 tbsp Soap Nut Liquid (p.47)
- 30ml/2 tbsp White Vinegar (p.24)
- 30 ml/2 tbsp surgical spirit
- 125ml/4½fl oz water
- 20 drops lemon essential oil (or other favourite – optional)

MAKES & KEEPS

Makes 200ml/7fl oz. Keeps 1 month.

METHOD

Put all the ingredients into a spray bottle and label. Shake well before use.

To use, apply the cleaner and wipe with a clean, soft cloth.

— Tip —

TO AVOID STREAKS,
DO NOT CLEAN WINDOWS WHEN
THEY ARE WARM – EARLY MORNING
OR DUSK IS THE BEST TIME.

Dirty Screen Cleaner

The uplifting lime gives it a pleasant aroma and adds to the cleansing effect.

INGREDIENTS
- 60ml/4 tbsp water (preferably distilled)
- 60ml/4 tbsp White Vinegar (p.24) or surgical spirit
- 10 drops lime essential oil

MAKES & KEEPS
Makes 125ml/4½ fl oz. Keeps 1 month.

METHOD
Simply mix all of the ingredients in a clean spray bottle.

To use, spray on a clean, lint-free cloth. Never spray liquid directly on a screen.

EMF Pollution Protector Screen Cleaner

The rosemary in this screen cleaner contains carnosic acid, which has been found to offer significant protection from mutagenic activity, so it can be protective against damage caused by radiation.

INGREDIENTS
- 60ml/4 tbsp water (preferably distilled)
- 60ml/4 tbsp White Vinegar (p.24) or surgical spirit
- 10 drops rosemary essential oil

MAKES & KEEPS
Makes 125ml/4½fl oz. Keeps 1 month.

Make and use in the same way as the Dirty Screen Cleaner.

Odour-busting Natural Drain Cleaner

The herbs and bicarbonate of soda control germs and help eliminate bad odours.

INGREDIENTS
- 15g/½oz dried thyme leaves, ground
- 15g/½oz dried rosemary leaves, ground
- 50 drops/½ tsp thyme essential oil
- 50 drops/½ tsp basil essential oil
- 1kg/2lb 3¼oz bicarbonate of soda

MAKES & KEEPS
Makes about 1kg/2lb 3¼oz. Keeps at least 1 year.

METHOD
Put the thyme and rosemary with the essential oils into a jar. Mix well. Add the bicarbonate of soda, then shake and stir to mix thoroughly. Store in a dry, airtight jar.

To use, first run the hot tap for a few minutes to warm up the drain. Then slowly pour about 1 teacup or half a mug of the scouring powder down the plughole. Dribble in a little hot water to send it down the pipe. Leave the cleaner to work overnight, then rinse to clear.

Lemon and Lime Natural Drain Cleaner

This zesty drain cleaner adds the deodorant and cleansing power of citrus to washing soda.

INGREDIENTS
- 250 g/1 cup washing soda
- Zest from 1 lemon or 1 lime
- 25 drops lemon essential oil
- 25 drops lime essential oil

MAKES & KEEPS
Makes 250g/1 cup. Keeps 2 months.

METHOD
Shake the washing soda and zest together in a jar to mix well. Add the essential oils and shake again. Store in an airtight container. (You can use the juice from the lemon and lime for cooking or drinks.) Use in the same way as the Odour-busting Drain Cleaner.

— Tip —
USE SOFT COTTON OR
FLANNEL CLOTHS FOR
POLISHING, ONES THAT DON'T
SHED THEIR FIBRES; I USE AN
OLD COTTON SHEET CUT UP.
MODERN MICRO-FIBRE
POLISHING CLOTHS ARE
ALSO GOOD.

Lemon Furniture Cleaner

With a great smell, this cleans and polishes dirty wood.

INGREDIENTS

- 200ml/7fl oz olive or linseed oil
- 20g/¾oz dried lemon balm or lemongrass (or 1 large handful of fresh)
- 120ml/4fl oz lemon juice (from about 4 lemons)

MAKES & KEEPS
Makes 300ml/10fl oz. Keeps 1 month.

METHOD
Make an infused oil with the oil and herbs (p.18). Mix the infused oil with the lemon juice and bottle.

Shake well before use. Rub well into wooden furniture or floors with a soft cloth. This mixture will also nourish your hands while you polish!

Spicy Furniture Cleaner

This variation cleans and polishes and gives a lovely warm, spicy smell as you polish.

INGREDIENTS

- 200ml/7fl oz olive, walnut or linseed oil
- 2 tbsp ground mixed spice
- 100ml/3½fl oz lemon juice, freshly squeezed or ready-prepared

MAKES & KEEPS
Makes 300ml/10fl oz. Keeps 2–3 months.

METHOD
Use the oil and mixed spice to make an infused oil (p.18). Add the lemon juice to the mixture and bottle.

Use in the same way as the Lemon Furniture Cleaner.

Lovely Furniture Polish

This solid polish is so nice to use that once you start polishing you can't stop!

INGREDIENTS
- 125ml/4½fl oz walnut oil
- 125ml/4½fl oz boiled linseed oil
- 40g/1⅜oz carnauba wax
- 30 drops lavender essential oil
- 30 drops eucalyptus essential oil

MAKES & KEEPS
Makes about 300ml/10fl oz. Keeps 6–12 months.

METHOD
Heat together the walnut and linseed oils and the carnauba wax in a water bath (p.21). When completely melted, remove from the heat, add the essential oils and pour into a jar or tin for storage. Apply to polished or unpolished wood with a lint-free cloth, and buff to a shine with a fresh cloth and some elbow grease.

Spicy Red Furniture Polish

I love the colour and smell of this one.

INGREDIENTS
- 125ml/4½fl oz infused hypericum oil*
- 20g/3 tbsp carnauba wax
- 10–20 drops cedarwood essential oil
- 10–20 drops cinnamon essential oil

MAKES & KEEPS
Makes 125ml/4½fl oz. Keeps 6–12 months.

METHOD
Make and use in the same way as the Lovely Furniture Polish.

*You can make an infused oil of hypericum using walnut, olive or linseed oil (p.18). It must be made with fresh flowers of St John's wort and left in the sun to infuse until it turns red (2–6 weeks).

Plant–based Wax for Raw Wood

Traditional recipes used beeswax added to an equal amount of turpentine and linseed oil. This veganized version substitutes carnauba wax, used at half the quantity because it is so much harder.

INGREDIENTS
- 80g/3oz carnauba wax in very small pieces
- 250ml/9fl oz turpentine
- 250ml/9fl oz boiled linseed oil
- 100 drops/1 tsp lavender essential oil

MAKES & KEEPS
Makes 750ml/1¼ pints. Keeps 2 years.

METHOD
In a bain-marie (p.21), melt the wax in the turpentine, then add the oil. In order to spread the wax easily, it needs to be warm, so you may need to reheat it before using; return it to your bain-marie if necessary.

Brush the warm wax mixture onto raw wood, working your way away from your starting point. The wood will absorb the wax as it dries. When it has dried completely after 30–60 minutes, buff it up into a shine with a soft cloth. The more you buff the wood, the shinier it gets. You can add more layers of wax to increase the shine.

> ## CAUTION
> Never leave heating oils unattended. Both turpentine and linseed oil are flammable at higher temperatures. Keep away from direct flame when applying.

Metal Polish

Clay and vinegar make a great polish for metals of all kinds.

INGREDIENTS
- 60ml/4 tbsp infused vinegar of your choice (p.18)
- 4 tbsp fine clay powder or fine earth from your own garden (but avoid stony or gritty soil, as it will scratch the metal)

MAKES & KEEPS
Makes 120ml/4fl oz. Keeps indefinitely.

METHOD
Mix the vinegar and earth together in a bowl.

Rub the polish on your metal ornaments with a damp cloth. Wipe off with a dry soft polishing cloth and enjoy the shine. I have used this on brass, silver and gold with good effect.

— Variation —
THIS METAL POLISH CAN BE MADE WITH LEMON JUICE INSTEAD OF INFUSED VINEGAR, IF DESIRED, BUT IT WILL KEEP IN THE FRIDGE FOR ONLY A WEEK.

Soap Nut Jewellery Cleaner

This effective recipe couldn't be simpler.

INGREDIENTS

- 50ml/3½ tbsp Soap Nut Liquid (p.47)
- 50ml/3½ tbsp distilled water

MAKES & KEEPS

Makes 100ml/3½fl oz. Use immediately.

METHOD

Mix the soap nut liquid and water together in a bowl. Place your jewellery into the mixture and leave to soak for 1 hour. Then gently scrub with a small soft brush (an old toothbrush will do), rinse well and dry.

—Tip—

USE THE JEWELLERY CLEANER
DILUTED WITH EQUAL PARTS OF
WATER IN AN ULTRASONIC CLEANER
FOR INCREDIBLE RESULTS.

Citrus Carpet Cleaner

This zesty carpet cleaner can also be diluted 1 part cleaner to 5 parts water (distilled is best) in a carpet shampooing machine and 50:50 in a steam cleaner. Always check the manufacturer's instructions before using with your carpet shampooing machine or steam cleaner.

INGREDIENTS

- 500ml/18fl oz distilled white vinegar or lemon-infused vinegar (p. 18)
- 25 drops/¼ tsp lemon essential oil
- 25 drops/¼ tsp orange essential oil
- 25 drops/¼ tsp lemongrass essential oil
- Bicarbonate of soda, as required

MAKES & KEEPS

Makes 500ml/18fl oz. Keeps indefinitely.

METHOD

Add the essential oils to the vinegar and mix well. Leave for a day before use.

To treat stains, make a paste with a little of the vinegar and a small amount of bicarbonate of soda. Stir before use. Brush well into the stained area (an old toothbrush is ideal for this job). Leave it to dry, then vacuum it up.

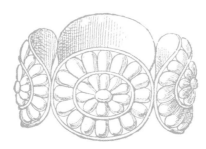

Pet Lover's Carpet Cleaner

The eucalyptus and lemon essential oils in this mixture are good to disguise pet smells, and the peppermint essential oil deters them from using the house as a toilet.

INGREDIENTS

- 125ml/4½fl oz lemon-infused vinegar (p.18)
- 250ml/9fl oz water
- 20 drops eucalyptus essential oil
- 20 drops lemon essential oil
- 20 drops peppermint essential oil

MAKES & KEEPS

Makes about 250ml/9fl oz. Keeps 2–3 months.

METHOD

Make and use in the same way as the Citrus Carpet Cleaner (opposite).

Steam Carpet Cleaner Mix

An elegantly simple eco-friendly carpet cleaner.

INGREDIENTS

- 60–120ml/2–4fl oz Soap Nut Liquid
- 10 drops peppermint essential oil

MAKES & KEEPS

Makes enough for one fill of steam cleaner. Use immediately.

METHOD

Mix the soap nut liquid and peppermint oil together. Add the mixture to the hot water in your steam cleaner and use as normal.

Soap Nut Liquid

This is the base recipe for making a soap nut liquid. Soap nuts are actually a fruit, not a nut! You can use the liquid on its own as a laundry liquid, or as an ingredient in a variety of recipes for cleaning around the house.

INGREDIENTS

- 20 soap nuts
- 2.5 litres/4½ pints water

MAKES & KEEPS

Makes about 750ml/1¼ pints. Keeps 1–2 weeks (you can also freeze the soap nut liquid in small containers and defrost as needed).

METHOD

Boil the soap nuts in 1.5 litres/2½ pints of water in a large saucepan for about 25 minutes. Add another 250ml/9fl oz of water and boil for another 20 minutes. After that, continue to add another 250ml/9fl oz of water every 10 minutes or so and boil for another 30 minutes. Strain into a sterilized container and keep in the fridge. Use 2-4 tbsp of liquid per load and wash as normal.

Citrus Odour-busting Upholstery Cleaner

Combining the gentle cleansing power of soap nuts with vinegar, the bubbles in the fizzy water used in this recipe help to lift off the dirt.

INGREDIENTS

- 125ml/4½fl oz sparkling water
- 60ml/4 tbsp White Vinegar (p.24)
- 30ml/2 tbsp Soap Nut Liquid (p.47)
- 4 drops orange essential oil
- 4 drops lemon essential oil

MAKES & KEEPS

Makes about 215ml/7½fl oz. Use immediately.

METHOD

Mix all ingredients together in a spray bottle.

Spray generously on to the upholstery, leave it to soak for 5 minutes, then scrub any stains in small circles to lift the dirt. Rinse with fresh water (or distilled if you live in a hard water area), then vacuum to remove the excess water. Alternatively, rinse with a steam cleaner. Ensure the area is thoroughly dried, otherwise there is a risk of mould or mildew developing.

—Tip—

YOU CAN USE A HAIRDRYER TO HELP DRY THE UPHOLSTERY.

Deep Clean Upholstery Cleaner

The bentonite clay used in the method draws out dirt and ingrained stains.

INGREDIENTS

Phase 1:

- 125ml/4½fl oz sparkling water
- 60ml/4 tbsp White Vinegar (p.24)
- 30ml/2 tbsp washing-up liquid or Soap Nut Liquid (p.47)
- 4 drops rosemary essential oil
- 4 drops lavender essential oil
- 4 drops juniper essential oil

Phase 2:

- Bentonite clay

MAKES & KEEPS

Makes about 215ml/7½fl oz. Use immediately.

METHOD

Mix the phase 1 ingredients in a spray bottle. Spray on to the upholstery and leave for 5 minutes. Then scrub in small circles to lift the dirt, especially stained areas. Rinse with fresh water, then vacuum or rinse with a steam cleaner.

For phase 2, make a paste from the clay by adding a little water. Spread the paste over the upholstery on any badly stained areas, working it in. Leave to dry, then vacuum it up. Ensure the area is thoroughly dried.

Leather Cleaner

Cleans and conditions your leather furniture while smelling gorgeous. It can also be used on leather bags, clothes and belts.

INGREDIENTS

- 125ml/4½fl oz White Vinegar (p.24)
- 1 slice of lemon
- 125ml/4½fl oz olive oil
- 30 drops lemon essential oil
- 10 drops mandarin essential oil

MAKES & KEEPS

Makes 250ml/9fl oz. Keeps 6 months.

METHOD

Use the vinegar and lemon slice to make a lemon-infused vinegar (p.18). Mix it in a storage bottle with the olive oil and essential oils.

Shake before use and apply in a circular motion onto leather. Leave for 20 minutes, then wipe with a clean cloth.

> **CAUTION**
>
> With any cleaning product, always apply to a small, inconspicuous area of furniture or carpet first before doing the whole thing.

Anti-mould Leather Furniture Cleaner

Cleans and protects with mould-busting plants and oils.

INGREDIENTS

- 125ml/4½fl oz coconut oil
- 125ml/4½fl oz olive oil
- 250ml/9fl oz lemon-infused vinegar (p.18)
- 20g/1 handful of thyme leaves
- 30 drops lemon essential oil
- 30 drops tea tree essential oil

MAKES & KEEPS

Makes 500ml/18fl oz. Keeps 6 months.

METHOD

Warm the coconut and olive oils in a bain-marie (p.21). Add the lemon-infused vinegar and essential oils and put into a storage bottle.

Warm and shake the bottle before each use. Apply in a circular motion to leather, leave for 1 hour and then wipe again with a clean cloth.

Mould-removing Spray for Walls

To reduce the reoccurrence of mould, do what you can to keep rooms dry and well ventilated. A dehumidifier can be a great investment if your building is damp.

INGREDIENTS
- 500ml/18fl oz White Vinegar (p.24)
- ½ tsp tea tree essential oil
- ½ tsp lemon essential oil

MAKES & KEEPS
Makes 500ml/2 cups. Keeps indefinitely.

METHOD
Mix the vinegar and essential oils in a spray bottle. Stand for 1 day before using. To use, spray generously over the area with the mould. Leave for an hour. Scrub gently off, then use some bicarbonate of soda on a cloth to wipe the walls clean. Make sure the walls dry out completely.

Bathroom Mould Spray

This is a two-phase treatment for bathroom mould. Do not use it on grout that hasn't been sealed or needs to be resealed.

INGREDIENTS

Phase 1:
- 500ml/18fl oz White Vinegar (p.24)
- ½ tsp tea tree essential oil
- ½ tsp clove essential oil
- ½ tsp thyme essential oil
- ½ tsp oregano essential oil

Phase 2:
- 1 tsp borax (see box, p.71)
- 1 tsp bicarbonate of soda
- 2 tsp lemon juice
- 250ml/9fl oz hot water

MAKES & KEEPS
Phase 1: makes 500ml/18fl oz.
Keeps indefinitely.
Phase 2: makes 300ml/10fl oz. Use immediately.

METHOD
Mix the phase 1 vinegar and essential oils in a spray bottle. Leave to brew for at least 1 day before using. Spray generously over the mouldy area. Leave for 1 hour.

Meanwhile, mix your phase 2 ingredients in a separate spray bottle. After the phase 1 mixture has been applied for 1 hour, wipe down and spray with the phase 2 mixture and scrub. Rinse thoroughly.

Spicy Laminate & Wooden Floor Cleaner

This mixture gives a lovely warm, spicy smell to your rooms. When cleaning laminate floors, make sure not to over-saturate the boards and to wipe up the spray right away. (Laminate floors don't like being wet.)

INGREDIENTS

- 250ml/9fl oz White Vinegar or Cider Vinegar (p.24)
- 2 cinnamon sticks, broken into pieces (or 15g/½oz ground cinnamon)
- 175ml/6fl oz surgical spirit
- 30ml/2 tbsp Castile-style Liquid Soap (p.65)
- 500ml/18fl oz warm water
- 50 drops/½ tsp orange essential oil

MAKES & KEEPS

Makes about 950ml/1¾ pints. Keeps at least 1 year.

METHOD

Use the vinegar and cinnamon sticks or ground cinnamon to make an infused vinegar (p.18). Add the surgical spirit, liquid soap, warm water and essential oil. Mix well and decant into a spray bottle for use.

Spray directly onto the floor and mop off with water.

Antibacterial Laminate & Wooden Floor Cleaner

This recipe is ideal for households with small children and pets.

INGREDIENTS

- 250ml/9fl oz White Vinegar or Cider Vinegar (p.24)
- 4g/⅛oz marigold petals
- 175ml/6fl oz surgical spirit
- 30ml/2 tbsp Castile-style Liquid Soap (p.65)
- 500ml/18fl oz warm water
- 50 drops/½ tsp thyme essential oil

MAKES & KEEPS

Makes about 950ml/1¾ pints. Keeps at least 1 year.

METHOD

Use the vinegar and marigold petals to make an infused vinegar (p.18). Add the surgical spirit, liquid soap, warm water and essential oil. Mix well.

Use in the same way as the Spicy Laminate & Wooden Floor Cleaner.

ROOM SPRAYS

Plant-based room sprays are widely used to freshen rooms. They play an important part in 'space-clearing' or 'energy-changing' exercises in the home.

To make the sprays, put the ingredients into a 100ml/3½fl oz spray bottle. Shake 24 times (a beneficial number in numerology to increase health and harmony in the home) to ensure the essential oils are mixed, then spray abundantly around the room. It can be fun to add a small, specially programmed crystal to the bottle. All except the Fly Repellent (p.56) make 100ml/3½fl oz and will keep for up to 3 months.

ROOM SPRAYS COURTESY OF LUCY HARMER.

Happy House Air Spray

A rich scent used to bring happiness and fun into a home, and to help relieve depression.

INGREDIENTS
- 100ml/3½fl oz spring water
- 12 drops basil essential oil
- 12 drops orange essential oil

Space Clearing Spray

*This refreshing and clean odour is said to clear 'heavy'
energy in the home.*

INGREDIENTS

- 100ml/3½fl oz spring water
- 14 drops juniper essential oil
- 14 drops lavender essential oil
- 14 drops rosemary essential oil

Computer Energy
Booster Spray

*The effect of these clear-smelling oils increases
concentration and boosts energy when you are
working on a computer.*

INGREDIENTS

- 100ml/3½fl oz spring water
- 8 drops lemon essential oil
- 8 drops lemongrass essential oil
- 8 drops pine essential oil

Helpful Angels Spray

Use when you are in need of divine assistance.

INGREDIENTS

- 100ml/3½fl oz spring water
- 8 drops frankincense essential oil
- 8 drops myrrh essential oil
- 8 drops sandalwood essential oil

Love Spray

To encourage love of all types into your life.

INGREDIENTS

- 100ml/3½fl oz spring water
- 8 drops rose essential oil
- 8 drops jasmine essential oil
- 8 drops sandalwood essential oil

Emotional Balancing Spray

For when life's ups and downs are getting to you.

INGREDIENTS

- 100ml/3½fl oz spring water
- 8 drops geranium essential oil
- 8 drops neroli essential oil
- 8 drops bergamot essential oil

Passion Spray

Speaks for itself!

INGREDIENTS

- 100ml/3½fl oz spring water
- 8 drops ylang ylang essential oil
- 8 drops patchouli essential oil
- 8 drops amber essential oil

Deep Sleep Spray

Zzzzzzzzzzzzz!

INGREDIENTS

- 100ml/3½fl oz spring water
- 12 drops lavender essential oil
- 6 drops chamomile essential oil
- 6 drops marjoram essential oil

Calm & Relaxation Spray

De-stress with this lovely spray.

INGREDIENTS

- 100ml/3½fl oz spring water
- 8 drops honeysuckle essential oil
- 8 drops cedar essential oil
- 8 drops vetivert essential oil

Protection Spray

*These plants were traditionally used to
protect the home against attacks or evil.*

INGREDIENTS
- 100ml/3½fl oz spring water
- 14 drops geranium essential oil
- 14 drops sage essential oil
- 14 drops petitgrain essential oil

Prosperity Spray

*This spray contains oils traditionally used
to attract wealth.*

INGREDIENTS
- 100ml/3½fl oz spring water
- 6 drops mint essential oil
- 6 drops cinnamon essential oil
- 9 drops vetivert essential oil
- 3 drops clove essential oil

—Tip—

THE ESSENTIAL OIL MIXES
WORK REALLY WELL IN HOME OIL
DIFFUSERS. ADD UP TO 6 DROPS IN
TOTAL TO 100ML/3½FL OZ OF WATER
INSIDE THE DIFFUSER.

Teenage Room Balancing Mucking Out Spray

This mix not only deodorizes but can help balance out tricky hormones.

INGREDIENTS

- 100ml/3½fl oz spring water
- 20 drops orange essential oil
- 20 drops ylang ylang essential oil
- 20 drops clary sage essential oil

Teenage Room Fragrant Mucking Out Spray

Teenage rooms can be particularly odorous.

INGREDIENTS

- 100ml/3½fl oz spring water
- 15 drops cypress essential oil
- 15 drops patchouli essential oil
- 15 drops cedarwood essential oil
- 15 drops rosemary essential oil

—Tip—

THESE SPRAYS ARE STRONGER
FOR MORE CONCENTRATED ODOUR
EATING, SO TAKE CARE TO AVOID
EYES AND SKIN WHEN SPRAYING,
AND DON'T USE THESE WHEN PETS
ARE IN THE ROOM.

Smokers' Odour Reduction Spray

It can be particularly effective to first 'smudge' your space with a sage smudge stick (p.112), then liberally spray everywhere with this lovely mix.

INGREDIENTS

- 100ml/3½fl oz spring water
- 20 drops rosemary essential oil
- 20 drops sage essential oil
- 20 drops patchouli essential oil

Fly Repellent

COURTESY OF TERI EVANS

This is a very strong mix to spray around doors and windows to repel flies and other insects. It is not for the body.

INGREDIENTS

- 50ml/3½ tbsp spring water
- 20 drops citronella essential oil
- 20 drops lavender essential oil

MAKES & KEEPS

Makes 50ml/1½fl oz. Keeps 3 months.

METHOD

Mix the water and essential oils together in a spray bottle.

Shake well, then spray around the window and door frames. Avoid contact with skin and eyes, as this is a strong mix.

POTPOURRI

Potpourri is a collection of dried or semi-dried herbs, flowers, woods and spices that is pleasant to the eye and gives off a lovely fragrance. Adding essential oils creates a stronger scent, and is also useful for refreshing the potpourri's fragrance.

To make any of these potpourris, mix the dried plant materials together in a beautiful bowl for display. Sprinkle the essential oils over the mix. See page 13 for how to dry your own plant material.

Each potpourri will keep well for 3–6 months. Refresh your mixture every so often with a few more drops of essential oils.

Devotees of Radha and Krishna (the Divine Couple of the Vedic tradition) offer flowers to Thakurji (the Divine in statue form). I like to make potpourri from these special prasaadam flowers. Prasaadam means 'mercy of God' – it gives you mercy or grace in the form of spiritual blessings.

Winter Festivities Potpourri

Collect together enough of the following to fill your chosen display bowl.

INGREDIENTS
- Holly leaves (handle with care!)
- Holly berries
- Cedar leaves
- Ivy leaves
- Small pine cones
- Pine needles
- Dried orange peel
- 1 tsp mint
- 1 nutmeg, freshly ground
- Glitter, to add some sparkle (optional)
- 10–20 drops cinnamon essential oil
- 10–20 drops orange essential oil
- 5–10 drops pine essential oil

Breathe-easy Potpourri

This potpourri can help with breathing difficulties.
Gather a mixture of the following to fill your bowl.

INGREDIENTS
- Pine needles
- Rosemary sprigs (broken into small pieces)
- Eucalyptus leaves
- Sage leaves
- Bay leaves
- Cedar leaves
- A few whole star anise
- 10–20 drops peppermint essential oil
- 10–20 drops clary sage essential oil
- 10–20 drops pine essential oil

Rainbow Potpourri

This will brighten up any room.

INGREDIENTS
- 2 handfuls of dried rose petals
  (red, pink, yellow and orange)

- A few of any of the following
  dried flowers and leaves:
  Marigolds
  Lavender
  Hydrangea
  Forget-me-nots
  Lemon balm
  Rosemary
  Sage

- 8 drops lavender essential oil
- 8 drops lemon balm essential oil
- 8 drops geranium essential oil
- 8 drops rose or rose geranium essential oil

Welcome Baby Potpourri

*With protective oils to celebrate and shelter
a new arrival.*

INGREDIENTS

- 2 handfuls of dried pink and yellow rose petals
- A few flowers from the hedgerow of the season
  the baby is born in – primroses, red campion,
  meadowsweet, heather – or berries in season
  – hawthorn, rowan, sloe
- 4 drops lavender essential oil
- 4 drops rosemary essential oil
- 4 drops juniper essential oil
- 4 drops rose or rose geranium essential oil

Happy House Potpourri

*What can be happier than a sunflower.
These beautiful flowers are easy to dry.*

INGREDIENTS

- 2 handfuls of dried red and yellow rose petals
- 1 dried sunflower head
- 1 handful of mixed dried rosemary and
  lemon balm leaves
- 8 drops basil essential oil
- 8 drops rosemary essential oil

Fruit & Spice Potpourri

*Collect together enough of the following to fill
a beautiful display bowl.*

INGREDIENTS

- Dried orange slices
- Dried lemon slices
- Dried grapefruit slices
- Dried pomegranate slices
- 1 tsp cloves
- 1 cinnamon stick, broken up
- 10–20 drops essential oil
- 10–20 drops orange essential oil

Valentine Potpourri

Love is in the air!

INGREDIENTS

- 2 handfuls of dried red and pink rose petals
- 1 handful of dried cherries or hawthorn berries
- 4 drops jasmine essential oil
- 4 drops sandalwood essential oil
- 4 drops ylang ylang essential oil
- 4 drops rose or rose geranium essential oil

—Tip—

TO DRY SLICES OF POMEGRANATE, LEMON,
GRAPEFRUIT AND ORANGE WITHOUT A
DEHUMIDIFIER, SLICE THEM THINLY AND PAT THEM
DRY WITH KITCHEN PAPER. PLACE ON GREASEPROOF
PAPER ON A BAKING TRAY, AND PUT INTO A COOL
OVEN – 140°C/275°F/GAS MARK 1 – FOR 1 HOUR,
TURNING OVER AFTER 30 MINUTES. REMOVE FROM
THE OVEN, PLACE ON CLEAN GREASEPROOF PAPER
AND LEAVE IN THE COOLEST OVEN FOR A FURTHER
2–3 HOURS, TURNING AFTER EVERY 30 MINUTES.

ECO LAUNDRY PRODUCTS

As every eco-conscious householder knows, modern detergents and laundry products contribute to serious environmental problems. These recipes offer green alternatives to washing soaps, liquids and powders, stain removers and fabric softeners as well as shoe treatments and moth repellents.

SOAP MAKING

You can buy the pure vegetable oil soap needed for the recipes in this book, or you can make your own from scratch. Making soap involves first preparing the lye, then separately warming and mixing an oil component, and finally combining these. Lye is a caustic substance so must be handled very carefully. Other ingredients are mostly added later (unless the recipe says otherwise). The cold-process recipes are for laundry soap, so they are stronger than some used on the body. The Lavender Laundry Soap (p.63) gives the instructions for cold-process solid soap making in full, and the Travellers' Anti-bug Laundry Soap (p.64) also refers to it. The third recipe is for a liquid soap that is made by a hot process, which is quite different.

Read the 'Key Techniques' section (pp.17–19) before commencing, read the instructions on the sodium hydroxide packaging before handling it, and make sure you are fully prepared, will not be disturbed, and children and animals will be kept away. Once underway, you cannot stop for some time. Soap will keep for several years.

FOR ALL RECIPES YOU WILL NEED

- Safety: overalls, gloves, protective glasses or goggles, a hair covering
- Vinegar or lemon juice to hand (to neutralize possible lye burns)
- Digital scales (accurate weighing is essential)
- Stainless steel or enamel saucepan (3–4-litre capacity)
- Silicone or stainless steel spatula/spoon
- Small stainless steel, glass or plastic bowls
- Bucket
- Liquid measuring cup

For cold-process solid soap making (opposite):
- A jam-making thermometer
- Moulds – either silicone soap moulds or a large mould (for example, a wooden box lined with plastic); if using the latter, you can cut the soap into bars later.

For hot-process liquid soap making (p.65):
- A slow cooker (one used only for soap)
- A handheld stick blender
- 1 or more containers with tight-fitting lids to store 4 litres of soap

---

CAUTION

Have all equipment ready before you start, including safety equipment. Soap making involves handling a dangerous chemical substance, so it needs extra caution. It helps to weigh or measure all the ingredients before you start, and have them safely stowed and ready to use.

Lavender Laundry Soap

COURTESY OF TANYA SMART

Handy for handwashing, stain removal and a travelling laundry solution, this cold-process soap is used grated in laundry liquid and powder recipes.

INGREDIENTS

- 400g/14oz water
- 140g/5oz sodium hydroxide
- 135g/4¾oz olive oil
- 180g/6⅜oz sunflower oil
- 620g/1lb 6oz coconut oil
- 5 tsp lavender essential oil

MAKES & KEEPS

Makes 12–14 small bars (about 115g/4oz each). Keeps several years.

METHOD

Take note of the safety measures in the general soap-making instructions (opposite) before preparing this recipe.

Pour the water into an appropriate container. Wearing gloves and plastic goggles, make the lye by carefully pouring the sodium hydroxide crystals into the container holding the water. Leave it to cool until 27–30°C/80–86°F. (Warning: NEVER pour water on to the lye, because this is very dangerous.)

Make an oil blend by gently heating the olive, sunflower and coconut oils until the coconut oil is melted, and cool until 27–30°C/80–86°F.

Carefully pour the lye into the oils and stir with the spatula until you reach 'trace' – a trace is when the movement of the spatula creates a line on the top of the mixture which doesn't disappear. It is a sign that your soap has reached full saponification – when the lye has turned the oils to soap – and indicates your mixture is ready. To reach trace usually takes about 30 minutes, but soap has its own timescale! Keep stirring continuously and very thoroughly, all around the sides and the bottom of the pan.

When you've achieved trace, you can add the essential oil. Ladle a little of the soap mixture into a bowl. Mix the essential oil into this small amount of soap mixture. Then mix this soap mixture back into the whole batch.

Next, pour the mixture into mould(s) and cover (you can use a piece of board with towels to insulate). Place the mixture out of the way for 24 hours.

After 24 hours, wearing gloves to protect against residual lye, remove the soap from the mould(s). Leave for another 24 hours to dry. You can then cut up the soap if you need to.

Wearing washing-up gloves (remember that the remnants will still be caustic), wash all your equipment with very hot water and lots of washing-up liquid, and rinse very thoroughly.

As with all soap, leave it to 'cure' in a well-ventilated place for 4–6 weeks. This ensures all the caustic effect of the lye has worn off.

Travellers' Anti-bug Laundry Soap

COURTESY OF TANYA SMART

This cold-press variation gives travellers extra protection from bugs and insects.

INGREDIENTS

- 400g/14oz water
- 140g/5oz sodium hydroxide
- 135g/4¾oz olive oil
- 180g/6⅜oz sunflower oil
- 620g/1lb 6oz coconut oil
- 2½ tsp lavender essential oil
- 100 drops/1 tsp cedarwood essential oil
- 100 drops/1 tsp juniper essential oil
- 50 drops/½ tsp basil essential oil

MAKES & KEEPS

Makes 12–14 average-sized bars.
Keeps years if well made, though the odour of the essential oils wears off.

METHOD

Follow the instructions for the Lavender Laundry Soap (p.63), taking note of the safety measures in the general soap-making instructions (p.62).

Prepare the lye first, then heat and cool the oil blend before adding the lye to it. Add the essential oils only after you have achieved trace.

Castile-style Liquid Soap

The hot process is used for making Castile-style liquid soap, an essential ingredient in many cleaning recipes. Traditionally, Castile soap is made from 100 per cent olive oil, but nowadays liquid soaps made from blended vegetable oils are often called 'castile' or 'Marseille' soap. This recipe is more strongly cleansing than one made purely from olive oil, so it is best for cleaning products.

INGREDIENTS

- 565g/1lb 4oz olive oil
- 400g/14oz sunflower oil
- 425g/15oz coconut oil
- 900g/2lb distilled water
- 270g/9½oz potassium hydroxide
- 2.3 litres/4 pints distilled water (separate from the lye)

MAKES & KEEPS

Makes around 5 litres/8¾ pints liquid soap. Keeps 1 year or more.

METHOD

Take note of the safety measures in the general soap-making instructions (p.62) before preparing this recipe.

Put the olive, sunflower and coconut oils into the slow cooker and turn it on to the low setting.

Meanwhile, make the lye. Do this outside, if possible, or by an open window. Put the 900g/2lb of distilled water into a large, stainless steel saucepan. Put on goggles and gloves. Pour the potassium hydroxide into the water carefully and slowly, without splashing. (Warning: NEVER pour the water into the lye, because this is very dangerous.)

Next, pour the lye-water mixture slowly and carefully into the oil in the slow cooker. Stir it with a spoon that can take the heat. The oil will become cloudy. Use a stick blender on slow to continue stirring carefully without splashing, until you have a 'trace'– a trace is when the movement of the spatula creates a line on the top of the mixture which doesn't disappear. You may need to stir for a long time – it can take anywhere from 5–10 minutes up to 40 minutes or more – and once started you cannot stop.

When you have a trace, put the lid on the slow cooker and leave it to heat (still on low). Stir and mix well every 20 minutes or so; don't worry if it separates – this is normal. Take care when you stir the mixture because it will still be corrosive. Fairly soon, it will become too thick to mix with the blender, so use a spoon or spatula instead. Eventually the mixture will start to resemble thick mashed potatoes and be difficult to mix.

Continue to stir every 20 minutes, until the mixture is translucent but yellowish. It can take up to 6 hours, but it may be ready in 4 hours. After 4–5 hours, test it by carefully dissolving 25g/1oz of the mixture into 50g/2oz very hot water in a clear glass container. Stir it: if it turns milky or cloudy, it needs to cook for longer; if it is clear, it's ready.

When it is ready, carefully weigh the thick paste (wearing gloves) and put it into a large saucepan. Bring the same quantity of water by weight (450g/1lb water to every 450g/1lb paste) almost to the boil and pour on top. Stir gently to dissolve. This can take a long time – you will need to stir, possibly heat it some more and stir again. If it keeps forming a whitish layer on top, dilute it more: add up to the same amount of water again and heat, stirring gently.

Store in large jars. Although I have used it immediately, it becomes more gentle with time, and I recommend leaving it to sit for 4–6 weeks to 'cure' before use.

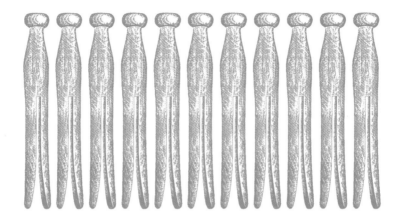

LAUNDRY LIQUIDS

To make these laundry liquids, first stir the washing soda into a little of the hot water in a bucket until it is dissolved. Then add the bicarbonate of soda (or borax, if using; see box p.71) and stir until dissolved. Mix in the liquid soap and stir gently to avoid too much frothing up. You can use more or less soap depending how hard or soft your water is. Experiment within the range to see what amount works best for you.

When all of these ingredients are dissolved, add the essential oils and the rest of the water. Stir gently, then funnel into storage bottles. If you don't have liquid soap, you can add 190–250g/6¾–8¾oz pure vegetable soap flakes or about half a bar of grated soap instead, dissolving it in a little boiling water before mixing in.

Shake well to mix before each use. For all these laundry liquids, with the exception of the Gentle Soap Nut Laundry Liquid (p.69), add 60–75ml/4–5 tbsp per load of washing to the compartment or drum.

Concentrated Lavender Laundry Liquid

For lavender linens.

INGREDIENTS
- 250g/8¾oz washing soda
- 4.5 litres/7¾ pints hot water
- 250g/8¾oz bicarbonate of soda or borax (borax makes a stronger mix, but bicarbonate of soda is better for people with sensitive skin; see box, p.71)
- 125ml–250ml/4½–9fl oz Castile-style Liquid Soap (p.65)
- 2 tsp lavender essential oil

MAKES & KEEPS
Makes 4.5 litres/7¾ pints.
Keeps at least 1 year.

— Tip —

ADD MORE LIQUID SOAP IF YOU NEED A STRONGER WASHING LIQUID. LIQUID CASTILE SOAP IS PREFERABLE, BUT IF YOU'RE UNABLE TO USE CASTILE, ANY LIQUID SOAP WILL DO.

Psoriasis-calming Laundry Liquid

Uses oils that are helpful for calming psoriasis.

INGREDIENTS

- 250g/8¾oz washing soda
- 4.5 litres/7¾ pints hot water
- 250g/8¾oz bicarbonate of soda
- 125ml/4½fl oz Castile-style Liquid Soap (p.65)
- 100 drops/1 tsp lavender essential oil
- 50 drops/½ tsp bergamot essential oil

MAKES & KEEPS

Makes 4.5 litres/7¾ pints.
Keeps at least 1 year.

Luxury Laundry Liquid

The finest essential oils give this a divine aroma.

INGREDIENTS

- 250g/8¾oz washing soda
- 4.5 litres/7¾ pints hot water
- 250g/8¾oz bicarbonate of soda or borax (borax makes a stronger mix, but bicarbonate of soda is better for people with sensitive skin; see box, p.71)
- 125ml–250ml/4½–9fl oz Castile-style Liquid Soap (p.65)
- 100 drops/1 tsp rose geranium essential oil
- 25 drops/¼ tsp neroli essential oil
- 25 drops/¼ tsp jasmine essential oil
- 10 drops rose essential oil (optional, as expensive)

MAKES & KEEPS

Makes 4.5 litres/7¾ pints.
Keeps at least 1 year.

Citrus Laundry Liquid

A traditional zesty one.

INGREDIENTS

- 250g/8¾oz washing soda
- 4.5 litres/7¾ pints hot water
- 250g/8¾oz bicarbonate of soda or borax (borax makes a stronger mix, but bicarbonate of soda is better for people with sensitive skin; see box, p.71)
- 125ml–250ml/4½–9fl oz Castile-style Liquid Soap (p.65)
- 100 drops/1 tsp lemon essential oil
- 50 drops/½ tsp grapefruit essential oil

MAKES & KEEPS

Makes 4.5 litres/7¾ pints.
Keeps at least 1 year.

Spicy Laundry Liquid

The cinnamon in this liquid gives a lovely warm smell. Nutmeg can also be used.

INGREDIENTS

- 250g/8¾oz washing soda
- 4.5 litres/7¾ pints hot water
- 250g/8¾oz bicarbonate of soda or borax (borax makes a stronger mix, but bicarbonate of soda is better for people with sensitive skin; see box, p.71)
- 125ml–250ml/4½–9fl oz Castile-style Liquid Soap (p.65)
- 100 drops/1 tsp lavender essential oil
- 50 drops/½ tsp orange essential oil
- 25 drops/¼ tsp cinnamon (or nutmeg) essential oil

MAKES & KEEPS

Makes 4.5 litres/7¾ pints.
Keeps at least 1 year.

Gentle Soap Nut Laundry Liquid

This liquid is suitable for babies and young children, wool and delicate fabrics.

INGREDIENTS

- 125ml/4½fl oz weak chamomile vinegar (made with 1 tsp chamomile flowers to 125ml/4½fl oz vinegar infused for 1 week, p.18)
- 60g/2oz soap nuts
- 1 litre/1¾ pints filtered or spring water
- 30 drops/⅓ tsp lavender essential oil
- 30 drops/⅓ tsp chamomile essential oil

MAKES & KEEPS

Makes around 600ml/1 pint. Keeps 6 weeks.

METHOD

Put the vinegar, soap nuts and water into a large lidded pan. Place over a medium heat and bring to a low boil. Simmer gently, covered, for 30 minutes.

Remove from the heat, mash the nuts (with a potato masher) and simmer, uncovered, for another 30 minutes, until the liquid reduces. Remove from the heat.

When cool, strain the liquid and press well before adding the essential oils, if using. Store in an airtight container.

To use, add around 60ml/4 tbsp per wash to your washing machine (use half this in a high-efficiency machine). As with all washing liquids, you can put it in the drawer of the machine or in the drum.

Pets' Bedding Laundry Liquid

Use this to discourage fleas.

INGREDIENTS

- 250g/8¾oz washing soda
- 4.5 litres/7¾ pints hot water
- 250g/8¾oz bicarbonate of soda or borax (borax makes a stronger mix, but bicarbonate of soda is better for people with sensitive skin; see box, p.71)
- 250ml/9fl oz Castile-style Liquid Soap (p.65)
- 100 drops/1 tsp lavender essential oil
- 50 drops/½ tsp tea tree essential oil

MAKES & KEEPS

Makes 4.5 litres/7¾ pints. Keeps at least 1 year.

METHOD

Mix gently before each use. Use 60–100ml/4–6 tbsp per load of washing.

Baby-soft Washing Powder

This is a very gentle mixture.

INGREDIENTS

- 250ml/9fl oz distilled white vinegar
- 1 tsp chamomile flowers
- 1 tsp rose petals
- 1 tsp lavender flowers
- 250g/8¾oz finely grated Lavender Laundry Soap (p.63) or other vegetable oil soap
- 250g/8¾oz bicarbonate of soda

YOU WILL NEED

- A food processor

MAKES & KEEPS

Makes about 750g/1lb 10½oz.
Keeps indefinitely in a sealed container.

METHOD

Use the vinegar, chamomile, rose and lavender to make an infused vinegar (p.18).

Put the grated soap into a large bowl. Stir in the washing soda and bicarbonate of soda. Gradually pour in the infused vinegar, a little at a time. This will make it foam up and thicken into a paste, so don't add it too quickly.

Whisk the mixture. You can do this by hand, but a food processor will be much easier, as it needs to be very thoroughly mixed. Whisk until it becomes a powder, then leave it to stand for 1 hour. The mixture will appear even more powdery, just like a washing powder. Stir again and store in a sealed (airtight) container.

You will need 2–3 tbsp for each full load of washing.

Super-strong Citrus Washing Powder

This recipe contains borax, which must be handled very carefully.

INGREDIENTS

- 1x100–120g/3½–4oz bar of laundry soap, grated (about 1 cup)
- 50 drops/½ tsp lemon essential oil
- 50 drops/½ tsp mandarin or orange essential oil
- 125g/½ cup washing soda
- 200g/7oz borax, if available (see box, opposite); if not, use another 125g/4½oz washing soda
- 125g/4½oz bicarbonate of soda

YOU WILL NEED

- A food processor

MAKES & KEEPS

Makes enough for 30–60 washes.
Keeps 6 months or more.

METHOD

Add the essential oils to the soap, then whisk or mix in a food processor to make a fine soap powder.

Add the washing soda, borax and bicarbonate of soda to the food processor, and mix all the ingredients well for 3–5 minutes.

To use, add 1–2 tbsp to the powder section of your washing machine drawer.

Space-clearer's Washing Powder

The essential oils in this recipe are used to cleanse and transform negative energy, so this powder is ideal for washing clothes before a space-clearing exercise.

INGREDIENTS

- 1 x 100–120g/3½–4¼oz bar of laundry soap, grated (about 1 cup)
- 50 drops/½ tsp lavender essential oil
- 50 drops/½ tsp rosemary essential oil
- 50 drops/½ tsp juniper essential oil
- 125g/4½oz washing soda
- 200g/7oz borax, if available (see box); if not, use another 125g/4½oz washing soda
- 125g/4½oz bicarbonate of soda

YOU WILL NEED

- A food processor

MAKES & KEEPS

Makes enough for 30–60 washes.
Keeps 6 months or more.

METHOD

Follow the instructions for the Super-strong Citrus Washing Powder (opposite).

Use 1–2 tbsp per wash.

—Tip—

BEFORE YOU USE THESE LAUNDRY POWDERS, DO ONE WASH WITH JUST A HALF MUG OF PLAIN WASHING SODA. THIS WILL CLEAN OUT ANY RESIDUES FROM YOUR OLD WASHING POWDER, WHICH COULD OTHERWISE REACT WITH YOUR HOMEMADE ECO-FRIENDLY MIX AND CAUSE A YELLOW COLOUR.

CAUTION

Borax, or sodium borate, is a naturally occurring mineral salt found in dry lake beds. It is a strong cleanser and whitener, and can treat mildew. Borax contains boron, a chemical that occurs in all vegetables and fruits not grown on exhausted soil, and one that is important for brain, bone and immune function. However, people with delicate, sensitive skin often find borax an irritant, and there is some evidence that it could be harmful to health, especially hormonal health, and the male reproductive system. Borax substitutes can be made from washing soda mixed with soap and vinegar, but bicarbonate of soda also works in the recipes. After researching this subject, I am happy to include borax in a recipe, but do research the subject yourself before making a decision. If you do use borax, as with any strong alkaloid, handle it with care; it can irritate the skin and should not be inhaled.

Conkers Detergent

*Said to be the European answer to soap nuts, conkers
from the horse chestnut tree can be used in similar ways,
although they are not as rich in saponins. This recipe
gives the simplest way to use them.*

INGREDIENTS

- 6 conkers, cut into quarters
- Small muslin bag

MAKES & KEEPS

Makes enough for 1 wash.
Can be used up to 3 times.
Dried conkers keep indefinitely.

METHOD

Simply put the pieces of conker into the bag
and place in the drum of the washing machine
with your wash.

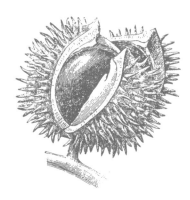

—Tip—

CUT YOUR CONKERS
(OR SMASH WITH A HAMMER)
WHEN THEY ARE FRESH,
THEN LAY OUT TO DRY TO KEEP
THEM ALL YEAR ROUND.

Soapwort Wool Wash

*The detergent power of this gentle washing liquid comes
from soapwort, which is easily grown in the garden.*

INGREDIENTS

- 60g/2oz dried soapwort leaves and stalks,
  or roots (or 120g/3 cups of fresh)
- 1 litre/1¾ pints water
- 250ml/9fl oz distilled white vinegar (or floral
  vinegar as for Baby-soft Washing Powder, p.70)
- 20 drops lavender or lemon essential oil
  (optional)

YOU WILL NEED

- A food processor

MAKES & KEEPS

Makes about 500ml/18fl oz. Keeps 1 year.

METHOD

Boil the soapwort leaves and stalks in the water for
approximately 10 minutes (if you are using roots, boil
for 20 minutes) with the lid on until the mixture has
reduced by one third. Leave to cool, then mix in a
blender (the liquid will become frothy). Leave it for a
few hours for the froth to die down, then strain well.

Add the white vinegar, or the floral vinegar if
you prefer a softer scent. Mix in the essential oil,
if desired.

Store in an airtight container. To use, add
120–180ml/½–¾ cup to your washing water.

Eco-powered Laundry Whitener

This fresh-smelling whitener relies on the bleaching power of lemon juice.

INGREDIENTS
- Juice of 5 lemons
- 1 litre/1¾ pints White Vinegar (p.24)
- 20 drops lemon essential oil

MAKES & KEEPS
Makes about 1 litre/1¾ pints. Keeps up to 6 months.

METHOD
Mix the ingredients together.

Add 125ml/4½fl oz of this whitener plus 60–125g/2–4½oz bicarbonate of soda to your regular washing liquid/powder, plus another 60–125ml/2–4½fl oz in the rinse compartment.

— Tip —

ANOTHER STAIN-REMOVAL METHOD
IS TO SCRUB UNDILUTED CASTILE-STYLE
LIQUID SOAP (P.65) INTO STAINS. LEAVE FOR
30–60 MINUTES AND WASH AS NORMAL.

Zesty Stain Remover

The basic principle of a stain remover is to use a concentrated amount of washing product. Try using this on colour-fast clothes.

INGREDIENTS
- 4 tbsp Super-strong Citrus Washing Powder or Baby-soft Washing Powder (p.70)
- Juice of 1 lemon

MAKES & KEEPS
Makes about 60ml/4 tbsp. Keeps 2–3 months.

METHOD
Mix a small amount – 1–2 tbsp – of your homemade washing powder with the lemon juice to make a paste. Then mix in the remaining washing powder. Store in a small jar.

As soon as you notice a stain, rub in a little of your stain-busting paste and put the item in the laundry basket, to await its normal wash. As with all stain removers, this remover is most effective if you treat the stain before it sets.

Wood Ash Detergent-free Washing Liquid

COURTESY OF MARC LUYCKX

Without the use of any detergent, this washing liquid is able to wash effectively in washing machines using a very strong alkaline product (potash or lye). Prepare it on a tiled floor and wear gloves and goggles while working with it.

INGREDIENTS

- Just over ½ bucket of sieved wood ash
- Boiling water

YOU WILL NEED

- A coffee filter

MAKES & KEEPS

Makes about ¼ bucket. Keeps indefinitely.

METHOD

Pour boiling water into the bucket until it reaches 4–5cm (1½–2in) above the ash. Mix it thoroughly, cover and leave to stand for 12 hours, stirring occasionally.

Stir, then filter through a piece of muslin. Carefully dispose of the ash (it is strongly alkaline) and rinse out the cloth and bucket.

Let the liquid settle, then place a sheet of kitchen paper, folded into four over the hole in a funnel. Add a coffee filter and strain the liquid through this into a solid plastic container. The liquid will be yellow to light brown in colour, but this will not affect clothes in any way (*Note: there are no suds*).

To use, put 125ml/4½fl oz of the washing product into the rinse compartment of your machine. Add 125ml/4½fl oz vinegar-based fabric softener (p.75) into the washing compartment.

For whitening: add an equal volume of washing soda and hot water, along with the washing liquid, to the washing compartment.

Note: for washes on 0–30°C/32–86°F, use half as much again of both liquid and vinegar.

CAUTION

While it is in theory possible to make your own potassium hydroxide lye, it is a highly dangerous operation that should not be attempted, as the strongly alkaline liquid can cause serious damage to eyes and skin.

SOFT–TOUCH HERBAL FABRIC CONDITIONERS

These easy-to-make fabric conditioners use a weak infused vinegar as their base. Vinegar, an acid, basically removes all traces of soap from the fabric, making it feel soft.

All these recipes make 1 litre/1¾ pints (enough for about 12 washes).

Skin-calm Fabric Softener

INGREDIENTS

- 1 litre/1¾ pints White Vinegar (p.24)
- 2 tbsp marigold flowers
- 50 drops/½ tsp lavender essential oil
- 50 drops/½ tsp bergamot essential oil
- A few drops rose essential oil (optional)

MAKES & KEEPS

Makes just over 1 litre/1¾ pints. Keeps 1–2 years.

METHOD

Use the vinegar and marigold flowers to make an infused vinegar (p.18). Add the essential oils to the infused vinegar.

To use, put about 80ml/5 tbsp into the rinse compartment of the washing machine.

Sweet & Soft Fabric Conditioner with Rose

INGREDIENTS

- 1 litre/1¾ pints White Vinegar (p.24)
- 1 tbsp fragrant rose buds or petals
- 50 drops/½ tsp lavender essential oil
- 25 drops/¼ tsp chamomile essential oil
- A few drops rose essential oil (optional)

MAKES & KEEPS

Makes just over 1 litre/1¾ pints. Keeps 1–2 years.

METHOD

Use the vinegar and roses to make an infused vinegar (p.18). Add the essential oils to the infused vinegar.

To use, put about 80ml/5 tbsp into the rinse compartment of the washing machine.

Antibacterial Fabric Softener

INGREDIENTS
- 1 litre/1¾ pints White Vinegar (p.24)
- 50 drops/½ tsp lavender essential oil
- 50 drops/½ tsp tea tree essential oil
- 25 drops/¼ tsp thyme essential oil

MAKES & KEEPS
Makes just over 1 litre/1¾ pints.
Keeps indefinitely.

METHOD
Mix all the ingredients together and bottle.

To use, put about 125ml/4½fl oz into the rinse compartment of the washing machine.

Pets' Bedding Fabric Conditioner

INGREDIENTS
- 1 litre/1¾ pints White Vinegar (p.24)
- 50 drops/½ tsp lavender essential oil
- 50 drops/½ tsp orange essential oil
- 50 drops/½ tsp tea tree essential oil

MAKES & KEEPS
Makes just over 1 litre/1¾ pints.
Keeps indefinitely.

METHOD
Make and use in the same way as the Antibacterial Fabric Softener.

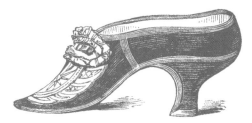

Shoe Odour Treatment

Good for smelly trainers!

INGREDIENTS

- 180g/6½oz bicarbonate of soda
- 120g/4¼oz cornflour
- 10 drops tea tree essential oil
- 10 drops eucalyptus essential oil
- 10 drops lemon essential oil
- 10 drops thyme essential oil

MAKES & KEEPS

Makes 300g/10½oz. Keeps up to 1 year.

METHOD

Put the powders into a sealed container and shake well to mix, then spread them out on a tray and sprinkle the oils over them. Return to the container for storage.

To use, fill a couple of small drawstring bags with the mix, put one in each shoe and leave for 12–24 hours. Repeat every few weeks or whenever you need to.

Between use, store them in an airtight container. You can use them many times, refreshing with more essential oils when the smell fades.

Smelly Shoe Spray

For a daily quick fix solution.

INGREDIENTS

- 250ml/9fl oz sage or witch hazel aromatic water (p.27)
- ½ tsp tea tree essential oil
- ½ tsp eucalyptus essential oil
- ½ tsp lemon essential oil
- ½ tsp thyme essential oil

MAKES & KEEPS

Makes 250ml/9fl oz. Keeps 1 year.

METHOD

Make a sage aromatic water by following the recipe for thyme aromatic water (p.28), substituting sage leaves for thyme leaves. Alternatively, use home-made or ready-made witch hazel (p.27). Pour the aromatic water into a spray bottle with the oils.

To use, shake well and spray shoes daily.

HERBAL MOTH REPELLENTS

Traditional moth balls can be toxic, so you might want to make your own plant-powered versions using dried herbs and essential oils.

To make each of the moth-repellent sachets, you will need a small piece of thin cotton cloth cut into a circle about 15cm (6in) in diameter, as well as silk or wool thread. Simply mix the dried herbs together in a bowl and sprinkle the essential oil, if using, over the mixture. Then lay your cloth on a flat surface and spoon half your herb mixture into the centre. Draw together the edges of the cloth and fasten tightly at the top with a piece of wool or silk thread.

Each of the moth-repellent recipes makes two sachets, which will keep for up to a year.

Before you pack clothes away for storing, make sure they are properly cleaned. Use a fabric conditioner as a rinse after washing. Air clothes well in the sun if you can before packing, then place these moth-repellent sachets between your folded clothes.

Lavender & Rosemary Moth Repellent

Traditional British recipe.

INGREDIENTS
- 2 tsp lavender flowers
- 2 tsp rosemary leaves and flowers
- 1 tsp thyme leaves
- 1 tsp cloves

Cedar & Southernwood Moth Repellent

A Mediterranean recipe.

INGREDIENTS
- 2 tsp small cedar wood shavings
- 2 tsp southernwood leaves
- 1 tsp cloves
- 1 tsp thyme leaves
- 20 drops lavender essential oil (optional)
- 20 drops cedar wood essential oil (optional)

Desert-style Moth Repellent

This one is inspired by the south-western deserts of the United States.

INGREDIENTS

- 2 tsp shredded sagebrush
- 2 tsp white sage
- 1 tsp cloves
- 1 tsp southernwood leaves
- 20 drops clove essential oil (optional)
- 20 drops sage essential oil (optional)

Spicy Moth Repellent

Mosquitoes don't like these ingredients either.

INGREDIENTS

- 2 tsp cinnamon sticks, broken up
- 8 bay leaves, broken up
- 2 tsp cloves
- 20 drops thyme essential oil
- 20 drops clove essential oil

Traditional Swiss Moth Repellent

This recipe comes from the Romandie (French-speaking) part of Switzerland and is made slightly differently.

INGREDIENTS

- Arolla pine (or other pine) wood shavings
- 15 drops arolla pine essential oil (a pine that only grows in the Swiss mountains at 1,300–2,500m /4,265–8,200ft)
- 15 drops larch essential oil

MAKES & KEEPS

Makes 1 pouch. Keeps variable time.

METHOD

Stuff a small drawstring bag with pine wood shavings sprinkled with the essential oils. Place in wardrobe or drawers where needed. Refresh the oils when they no longer smell.

GARDEN & HOUSE PLANT CARE

Plants not only have a lot to offer to help our home and us, but also each other. Here are recipes for protecting, nourishing and caring for plants in your home and garden.

Pungent Pest Control Spray for Plants

Controls pests on outdoor or indoor plants without harming the plant.

INGREDIENTS
- 6 large fresh chillies
- 500ml/18fl oz water
- 1 head garlic, peeled and crushed

MAKES & KEEPS
Makes nearly 500ml/18fl oz. Keeps about 1 week in the fridge.

METHOD
Boil the chillies in the water for 15 minutes. Add the garlic and steep for several hours or overnight. Strain well through a piece of muslin and pour into a spray bottle, ready to use.

Spray any affected plants thoroughly, coating the leaves, stalks and earth.

Tobacco & Tea Tree Plant Spray

An effective remedy against many insects.

INGREDIENTS
- 500ml/18fl oz boiling water
- 1 handful of tobacco (such as a cheap pipe tobacco)
- 100 drops/1 tsp tea tree essential oil

MAKES & KEEPS
Makes nearly 500ml/18fl oz. Keeps about 5 days in the fridge.

METHOD
Pour the boiling water over the tobacco. Leave to cool. Strain, add the tea tree essential oil and pour into a spray bottle.

Spray any affected plants.

CAUTION
Best used outside. Take care when spraying, as the chilli can really sting if it gets up your nose or in your eyes. Keep away from children or pets.

Antifungal Plant Spray

For fungal infections including black spot and powdery mildew.

INGREDIENTS

- 15ml/1 tbsp neem oil
- Hot water
- 1 heaped tsp bicarbonate of soda
- 1 tsp Castile-style Liquid Soap (p.65)
- 20 drops lemon essential oil
- Up to1 litre/1¾ pints water

MAKES & KEEPS

Makes up to 1 litre/1¾ pints. Use immediately.

METHOD

Mix the neem oil with some very hot water and bicarbonate of soda, then add the liquid soap and lemon oil. Mix and add a little cold water, then gradually add more cold water, stirring, up to 1 litre/1¾ pints.

Spray the leaves of infected plants.

Horseradish Antifungal Plant Treatment

A fiery vinegar plant treatment.

INGREDIENTS

- 125ml/4½fl oz Cider Vinegar (p.24)
- 25g/1oz fresh horseradish, grated (use dry powder if you can't find fresh)

MAKES & KEEPS

Makes 125ml/4fl oz. Keeps 6 months.

METHOD

Use the vinegar and horseradish to make an infused vinegar (p.18).

To use, add 45ml/3 tbsp to 1 litre/1¾ pints of water and spray your plants. Repeat every few days.

Soap Nuts Antibug Spray

This spray for indoor and outdoor plants can also be used on the skin as a bug repellent.

INGREDIENTS

- 250ml/9fl oz Soap Nut Liquid (p.47)
- 15 drops citronella or lemongrass essential oil
- 15 drops cedarwood essential oil
- 15 drops tea tree essential oil

MAKES & KEEPS

Makes 250ml/9fl oz. Keeps up to 1 week.

METHOD

Pour the soap nut liquid into a spray bottle and mix in the essential oils.

Spray on any affected plants regularly.

Houseplant Bug Spray for Spider Mites

This is specific for red spider mites, which can devastate plants.

INGREDIENTS

- 2 large handfuls of fresh coriander
- 500ml/18fl oz Cider Vinegar (p.24)
- 15ml/1 tbsp neem oil
- 45ml/3 tbsp surgical spirit
- Bicarbonate of soda

MAKES & KEEPS

Makes 350ml/12fl oz. Keeps 1 year.

METHOD

Use the coriander and vinegar to make an infused vinegar (p.18). Separately, mix the neem oil with the surgical spirit, leaving the mix to infuse.

After 1 month, strain the vinegar and mix it with the neem oil-surgical spirit mix in a bottle.

To use, add 60ml/4 tbsp of the combined mix to 250ml/9fl oz of water plus a tsp of bicarbonate of soda in a spray bottle.

Super-organic Plant 'Manure'

This recipe makes an effective but very smelly plant food.

INGREDIENTS
- 5 handfuls of fresh comfrey leaves
- 5 handfuls of fresh stinging nettles (wear gloves!)

MAKES & KEEPS
Makes a variable amount. Keeps indefinitely.

METHOD
Simply put the fresh comfrey and nettles into a bucket and fill the bucket with water. Leave it in a corner of the garden with a loose-fitting lid.

No need to strain it, just start to use after a month. Add 1–2 tbsp of the black liquid to 1 litre/1¾ pints of water and feed your plants.

Happy Houseplants Comfrey Feed

This is a comfrey food that can be made and used immediately, and it doesn't have an off-putting smell, so it can be used for indoor plants too.

INGREDIENTS
- 1 handful of fresh comfrey leaves, chopped
- Up to 500ml/18fl oz water

MAKES & KEEPS
Makes a variable amount. Keeps indefinitely.

METHOD
Blend the comfrey and water in an electric blender until completely smooth. Store in an airtight container.

Add 1 tbsp to 1 litre/1¾ pints of water for watering houseplants. After 2 weeks, it will start to smell stronger, and at some point it will be too smelly for indoor plants – but it will still be good for outdoor plants.

Antifungal Seedling Spray

A gentle spray for baby plants.

INGREDIENTS
- 1 handful of fresh chamomile (or 3 teabags)
- 500ml/18fl oz boiling water
- 1 tsp tea tree essential oil

MAKES & KEEPS
Makes 500ml/18fl oz. Keeps 1 week.

METHOD
Use the chamomile and boiling water to make a chamomile infusion (p.17), leaving it to cool overnight before straining. Stir in the tea tree oil and pour into a spray bottle.

Spray seedlings lightly every day when they are not in full sun.

Orchids' Pub Lunch

It seems that many houseplants, especially orchids, like beer.

INGREDIENTS
- 200ml/7fl oz Cider Vinegar (p.24)
- 15g/½ oz dried comfrey
- 250ml/9fl oz real ale (unpasteurized cloudy beer)
- 240g/8½oz Epsom salts
- 500ml/18fl oz water

MAKES & KEEPS
Makes 1 litre/1¾ pints. Keeps up to 1 year.

METHOD
Use the vinegar and comfrey to make an infused vinegar (p.18). Mix this vinegar with the remaining ingredients in an airtight container.

Feed each plant 15ml/1 tbsp every week after watering.

Humane Slug Repellent

A vegan approach to this pesky gardeners' problem.

INGREDIENTS
- Used ground coffee
- Orange peel

MAKES & KEEPS
Makes a variable amount.
Keeps 1 week.

METHOD
First, sprinkle the coffee around your vegetables, using it to make a thick boundary to protect them. Lay the orange peel close by to attract any slugs. You can then easily remove them from the peel and liberate them into the wild – far from your garden.

— Tip —

A NATURAL WAY OF DETERRING INSECTS IS TO PLANT PLENTY OF DETERRENT PLANTS AMONGST YOUR VEGETABLES AND FLOWERS – TRY CHRYSANTHEMUMS, LEMONGRASS, MARIGOLDS, BASIL, LAVENDER, THYME, CATNIP, MINT AND TOBACCO.

ON THE ROAD

Eco-conscious car enthusiasts will love these simple and cheap-to-make screen-washes that are kinder alternatives to harsh detergents. Make your car shine with plant-powered polishes and traditionally made waxes, and smell great with homemade air fresheners.

Eco-friendly Sudsy Car Soap

A soapy mix that is perfect for washing the car.

INGREDIENTS
- 250ml/9fl oz Castile-style Liquid Soap (p.65)
- 4 tbsp laundry powder

MAKES & KEEPS
Makes 1 wash. Use immediately.

METHOD
Mix the liquid soap and laundry powder together in a large bucket of water.

Wash the car with the mixture. Rinse well, then use Plant-powered Car Wax (p.87).

Mint Screen Wash

An Earth-friendly windscreen wash for your car.

INGREDIENTS
- 250ml/9fl oz White Vinegar (p.24)
- 5ml/1 tsp Castile-style Liquid Soap (p.65)
- 50 drops/1 tsp peppermint essential oil
- Green food colouring (optional)
- 2 litres/3½ pints water

MAKES & KEEPS
Makes 2.25 litres/4 pints.
Keeps 2 months.

METHOD
Mix all the ingredients together in a large container. Shake well and pour into the windscreen wash container of your car.

Plant-powered Car Wax

This citrus wax uses carnauba – a rich, thick wax from the leaves of the carnauba palm from Brazil.

INGREDIENTS

- 125ml/4½fl oz White Vinegar (p.24)
- 125ml/4½fl oz turpentine
- Peel from 1 lemon
- Peel from 1 orange
- 250ml/9fl oz linseed oil
- 55g/2oz carnauba wax
- 1 tbsp coconut oil
- 1 tsp mixed orange and lemon essential oils (optional)

MAKES & KEEPS

Makes about 500ml/18fl oz.
Keeps indefinitely.

METHOD

Put the vinegar, turpentine and lemon and orange peels into a jar and seal to make an infused vinegar/turpentine (p.18). Leave to infuse for 2–3 weeks.

Put the infused vinegar/turpentine into a bain-marie along with the linseed oil, carnauba wax, coconut oil and essential oils, if using, and heat gently until the wax has melted. Stir rapidly and pour into a heat-resistant container.

When the mixture is cool, it will become very solid. Rub it onto the car with a lint-free cloth. Polish to a deep shine with the corner of a cotton duster soaked in vinegar.

Plant-powered Tyre Shine

This tyre shine makes your tyres look great and conditions the rubber.

INGREDIENTS
- 300ml/10fl oz castor oil
- 15ml/1 tbsp lemon essential oil

MAKES & KEEPS
Makes 315ml/10½fl oz. Keeps 1 year.

METHOD
Mix the oils in a suitable storage bottle.

To use, apply to clean, dry tyres with a cloth, polishing with a circular motion for maximum shine.

Dashboard Clean & Polish

Make your dashboard look as good as new with this lovely-smelling polish.

INGREDIENTS
- 125ml/4½fl oz coconut oil
- 50 drops/½ tsp lemon oil

MAKES & KEEPS
Makes 125ml/4½fl oz. Keeps up to 1 year.

METHOD
Warm up the coconut oil in the sun, on a radiator or by placing the jar in a bain-marie and heating for 2–4 minutes. Mix the lemon oil into the coconut oil and store in a small jar covered with a lid.

To use, first clean the dashboard using an eco-friendly cleaner (pp.26–8) and dry with a towel. Apply a small amount of polish with a damp sponge, and rub in.

—Tip —

Winter Screen Wash

In the cold months, add alcohol to prevent the windscreen wash freezing. Adjust the levels of water and alcohol depending on how cold it is, so that more alcohol is used as the temperature drops.

INGREDIENTS

- 125ml/4½fl oz White Vinegar (p.24) or a lemon-infused vinegar (p.18)
- 60–250ml/2–9fl oz surgical spirit
- 2 tsp Castile-style Liquid Soap (p.65)
- 50 drops/1 tsp lemon essential oil
- Up to 2 litres/3½ pints water

MAKES & KEEPS

Makes about 2.5 litres/4½ pints. Keeps 2 months.

METHOD

Make and use in the same way as the Mint Screen Wash (p.86).

CAR AIR FRESHENERS

For these recipes, you will need a small cotton bag, around 5 x 12cm/2 x 8in, with a drawstring top, or the materials to make one. Simply fill the bag with the solid material and sprinkle on 20–30 drops of the essential oils. The recipes suggest blending 10ml/2 tsp of oils, but keep the remainder in the glove compartment to refresh the pouch weekly. Hang the pouch up or keep it somewhere in the car.

Each recipe makes one pouch and keeps a variable time.

Smokers' Car Freshener

Odour-reducing to clear tobacco smells.

INGREDIENTS

- 115–215g/4–7½oz bicarbonate of soda
- ⅔ tsp lemon essential oil
- ⅔ tsp eucalyptus essential oil
- ⅔ tsp patchouli essential oil

Stay Awake
Car Air Freshener

A stimulating mix to help you stay awake on long journeys.

INGREDIENTS
- 45g/1½oz fresh ground coffee
- 100 drops/1 tsp rosemary essential oil
- 100 drops/1 tsp coffee essential oil

Relaxed Driver Car Scent

This is perfect for nervous drivers.

INGREDIENTS
- 15g/½oz chamomile flowers
- 15g/½oz lavender flowers
- 25 drops/¼ tsp rose otto essential oil
- 25 drops/¼ tsp clary sage essential oil
- 25 drops/¼ tsp ylang ylang essential oil
- 25 drops/¼ tsp melissa essential oil

Happy Dog
Air Freshener

These scents are proven by research to make dogs relaxed and sleepy. Find a place in your car to put the pouch out of reach of your dog.

INGREDIENTS
- 25g/1oz dried valerian
- 15g/½oz dried strips of coconut
- 100 drops/1 tsp vanilla essential oil
- 100 drops/1 tsp ginger essential oil

Smelly Dog Seat Cleaner

The perfect car upholstery cleaning spray to freshen up your car seats and remove doggy smells.

INGREDIENTS
- 125ml/4½fl oz White Vinegar (p.24)
- 125ml/4½fl oz surgical spirit
- Peel from 2 lemons
- 250ml/9fl oz filtered water
- 50 drops/½ tsp eucalyptus essential oil
- 50 drops/½ tsp lavender essential oil

MAKES & KEEPS
Makes 500ml/18fl oz. Keeps indefinitely.

METHOD
Use the vinegar, surgical spirit and lemon peel to make a combined tincture/infused vinegar (p.18).

After it has infused, pour it into a spray bottle with the water and essential oils and leave overnight. You can start to use it the next day.

To use, shake well then spray on to car seats and wipe with a clean, dry cloth. Leave to dry.

Hedge-witch Herbal Car Protection Charm

Make a car protection charm with 3 or more of these herbs traditionally used for magical protection.

INGREDIENTS
- 1 tsp dried agrimony
- 1 tsp dried rue
- 1 tsp dried mugwort
- 1 tsp dried sage
- 1 tsp rosemary
- 1 tsp cedar
- Dragon's blood

YOU WILL NEED
- A small cloth pouch

MAKES & KEEPS
Makes 1 charm. Keeps 12 months.

METHOD
Choose 3 of the herbs in the list and mix together, then fill a small cloth pouch with them and sew it shut. While you work, visualize your car as completely protected. Hang the pouch up in your car or hide it in the glove compartment.

PETS' CORNER

Many a happy home comes complete with companion animals. Here are a few simple recipes to help keep you and your furry friends happy.

Anti-scratch Carpet Treatment

This simple recipe helps you train your cat not to sharpen their claws on your carpets. Cats need to scratch, so always make sure they have a scratching post or mat as an alternative.

INGREDIENTS
- 50g/2oz ground pepper
- 50g/2oz dried rue, ground to a fine powder

MAKES & KEEPS
Makes 100g/3½oz. Keeps 1 year.

METHOD
Mix the ground pepper and rue into a shaker with holes in the top. Sprinkle some of the powder on the carpet where the cats like to scratch.

WARNING
Not suitable for very light-coloured carpets.

Purr-fect Wheatgrass

Cats adore grass and like to nibble on it to keep them healthy. Keep your furry friends in fine fettle with this lovely addition to your home.

INGREDIENTS
- 1 packet wheatgrass seeds or oat seeds

YOU WILL NEED
- A small flowerpot
- Organic potting compost

MAKES & KEEPS
Makes a variable amount. Keeps indefinitely.

METHOD
Fill your pot with organic potting compost to 5cm/2in from the top. Scatter a handful of grass seed over the top in a thin layer, then add more compost to cover the seeds with a 5mm/¼in layer. Water to moisten the soil.

Cover with a piece of glass or clear plastic, allowing some airflow, and put the pot somewhere warm and dark, where the cats can't get to it. Check it every 2–3 days, keeping it moist.

Sprouts will appear from day 2 or 3. When the sprouts are up to the level of the cover (usually by day 3 or 4), remove the cover and move the pot to a sunny spot (still away from the cats).

After a week or more when the grass is 10–15cm/4–6in tall, you can put the pot where the cats can reach it and enjoy watching them nibble it.

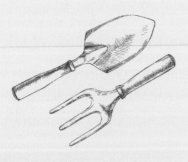

Catslick

Cats love the smell of the herb valerian, so you can make them very happy with it. This is for any cat, and is particularly useful for washing old and sick cats who can no longer care for their own fur.

INGREDIENTS

- 150g/5oz valerian dried root or 300g/10½oz fresh root
- 2.5 litres/4½ pints water
- 15-30 drops lavender essential oil (optional)
- 15-30 drops chamomile essential oil (optional)

MAKES & KEEPS

Makes 300ml/10½fl oz. Keeps at least 1 year.

METHOD

Use the valerian and water to make an aromatic water in the same way as the Witch Hazel Aromatic Water (p.27), cooking them for 30 minutes in the pressure cooker to start, then leaving to cool and reheating with the tubing attachment to make the distilled water. Store in a bottle and add the essential oils, if using.

Apply small amounts to cotton pads and gently wipe your cat's fur.

Happy Rabbit Herbs

These herbs are enjoyed by rabbits and are beneficial to their health. For optimum health, rabbits need to eat fresh plants every day.

INGREDIENTS

Living plants:
- Dandelion
- Garlic mustard
- Chamomile
- Rosemary
- Lemon balm

MAKES & KEEPS

Makes a variable amount. Keeps indefinitely.

METHOD

For any or all of the plants listed above, buy small plants, grow from seed or collect from the wild.

Keep your rabbit happy with a handful of fresh leaves daily.

Calm Dog

Dogs have a very acute sense of smell, and odours have strong and particular effects on them.

INGREDIENTS
- 50g/2 oz dried valerian root
- 2 vanilla pods
- 250ml/9fl oz vodka

MAKES & KEEPS
Makes 250ml/9fl oz. Keeps up to 1 year.

METHOD
Chop the valerian root and add it with the vanilla pods to the alcohol in a lidded jar to make a tincture (p.17). Strain and bottle.

To use, apply drops of the scent to cloths placed in your dog's bed and favourite places, or in the car when travelling.

Sleepy Dog

The odours of these plants have been found to make dogs sleep more.

INGREDIENTS
- 25g/1oz freshly grated coconut, or dessicated coconut
- 25g/1oz freshly grated ginger, or ground ginger
- 250ml/9fl oz vodka

MAKES & KEEPS
Makes 250ml/9fl oz. Keeps indefinitely.

METHOD
Use the coconut, ginger and alcohol to make a tincture (p.17). This gives you a coconut and ginger essence.

To use, apply drops of the scent to cloths placed in your dog's bed or favourite spots, or in the car when travelling.

—Variation—
IN PLACE OF THE VALERIAN AND VODKA TINCTURE, YOU COULD USE A VALERIAN AROMATIC WATER (P.27).

Dogs' Paradise

Dogs love to nibble on plants in the garden or from pots, perhaps as a way of self-medicating to keep healthy.

INGREDIENTS

Living plants:
- Chamomile
- Peppermint
- Basil
- Oregano
- Parsley

MAKES & KEEPS

Makes a variable amount. Keeps indefinitely.

METHOD

For any or all of the plants listed above, buy small plants, or grow from seed. Grow them in your garden or in pots outside, or in a large heavy pot indoors – a heavy pot means your dog can nibble at it without knocking it over!

Allow your dog to nibble on the leaves whenever it wants.

Neem & Calendula Skin Salve

This useful healing and calming skin salve can be used on dogs as well as other animals, including humans.

INGREDIENTS
- 1 handful of fresh calendula (English marigold) flowers
- 200ml/7fl oz olive oil
- 100ml/3½fl oz neem oil
- 25g/1oz grated beeswax

MAKES & KEEPS

Makes 250ml/1 cup. Keeps at least 1 year.

METHOD

Gently heat the calendula flowers and olive oil to make an infused oil (p.18). The liquid will turn orange, the colour of the flowers. Strain the mixture then gently heat the neem oil and beeswax with the calendula-infused oil to make a salve.

Apply liberally and frequently to infected skin.

INKS, PAINTS & DYES

The plant world yields many beautiful natural colours, some temporary and of use for children's artwork or practice painting. Others are true dye plants and can be worked with to make permanent colours for inks, paints and dyes.

Blue-purple Ink

The colour comes from berries.

INGREDIENTS

- 2 handfuls of ripe elderberries (or bilberries/ huckleberries)
- 4 tbsp White Vinegar (p.24)
- ½ tsp benzoin (Friars' Balsam) tincture or myrrh tincture
- 5 drops thyme or rosemary essential oil
- 1 tsp gum arabic for each 60ml/4 tbsp of dye

MAKES & KEEPS

Makes about 60ml/4 tbsp. Keeps around 6 months.

METHOD

Simmer the berries in the vinegar, mashing with a potato masher and stirring to prevent burning, for 15 minutes. Strain and press through a piece of muslin to get all the juice out (wear gloves as this juice seriously stains).

Mix the other ingredients with the dye liquid and bottle.

Use the ink for painting or for writing with a dipping pen and inkwell.

Brown Ink

COURTESY OF TERI EVANS

INGREDIENTS

- 6–8 whole walnuts, gathered from the ground when blackened with age
- 125ml/4½fl oz water
- 125ml/4½fl oz White Vinegar (p.24)
- 5ml/1 tsp benzoin (Friars' Balsam) tincture or myrrh tincture
- 5 drops thyme or rosemary essential oil
- 1 tsp gum arabic for each 60ml/4 tbsp of dye

MAKES & KEEPS

Makes about 60ml/4 tbsp. Keeps up to 1 year.

METHOD

Simmer the walnuts in the water for 30 minutes to 1 hour, topping up with the vinegar as the water boils away. You should end up with 60–120ml/2–4fl oz of dark brown liquid.

Strain the liquid and press through a piece of muslin (use gloves and take care as this dye will seriously stain). Mix the other ingredients with the liquid and bottle.

Use in the same way as the Blue-purple Ink.

Black Acorn Ink

COURTESY OF LUCY WELLS

Acorns will yield a black ink for writing and drawing.

INGREDIENTS

- 400g/14 oz acorns (about 4 handfuls)
- 25ml/5 tsp Rust Water (p.106)
- 1 tsp gum arabic for each 60ml/4 tbsp of dye

MAKES & KEEPS

Makes variable amount. Keeps up to 1 year.

METHOD

Put the acorns into a saucepan full of water and simmer for 3–7 days, turning off at night and back on in the day, and topping up with water so the acorns are always covered. Strain the liquid off and boil it some more to reduce it to half, then add the rust water and gum arabic and bottle.

Note: Gum arabic is a natural gum made of hardened sap from two species of acacia tree: senegalia and vachellia.

Iron Gall Ink

COURTESY OF LUCY WELLS

This is a very ancient recipe using galls – the small woody balls that grow on oak trees, which are made by insects living inside them. They are very rich in tannins and give them up more readily than acorns. The added iron ensures a black colour.

INGREDIENTS

- 2 handfuls of oak galls, broken up
- Rust Water (p.106)
- 1 tbsp gum arabic for each 60ml/4 tbsp of dye
- Surgical spirit or benzoin (Friars' Balsam) tincture

MAKES & KEEPS

Makes variable amount. Keeps up to 1 year.

METHOD

In a saucepan, boil the broken up oak galls in enough water to cover for 1 hour then leave to soak overnight.

The next day, heat again for 1 hour, then turn off the heat and add enough rust water so that the liquid is a very dark black and sufficient gum arabic. Add 25 per cent surgical spirit or Friars' Balsam to preserve, and bottle.

Vegan Wax 'Varnish'

A wood treatment that can be applied to raw wood or over a wood stain for a totally natural alternative to gloss and satinwood paints.

INGREDIENTS
- 160g/5½oz wax
- 250ml/9fl oz linseed oil
- 750ml/1¼ pints tung oil
- 500ml/18fl oz turpentine
- 1 tbsp orange oil

MAKES & KEEPS
Makes 1.5 litres/2½ pints. Keeps indefinitely.

METHOD
Melt the wax and linseed oil together in a bain-marie. Turn the heat down and add the tung oil, stirring. Remove from the heat and stir in the turpentine and orange oil, stirring continuously.

To use, brush on to wood while the oil is still warm. Leave to soak in, then polish. Applying multiple thin layers works best, with 1–2 days in between. Heat to re-melt when it starts to set. If doing a large area, such as a floor, use a portable camping stove so you can move the pan around as you work.

WOOD STAINS

You can make a plant-based wood stain using a water decoction (p.17) or an infused vinegar (p.18). These recipes make 750ml/1¼ pints of wood stain and keep 6–12 months. To use, paint thinly on bare wood and apply repeated coats for deeper shades. Coat with Vegan Wax 'Varnish' for a shiny, finished look.

Grey Wood Stain

The addition of rust water turns the brown of the tea to a lovely grey.

INGREDIENTS
- 8–12 teabags
- 750ml/1¼ pints White Vinegar (p.24)
- 5–20/1–4 tsp Rust Water (p.106)

METHOD
Put the teabags with the vinegar in a lidded jar and leave to stand for 1–3 weeks. After it has infused, strain and add the rust water – the more you add the darker the grey. Alternatively, simply put a few rusty nails into the vinegar and teabag brew at the beginning.

Khaki Green Wood Stain

Onions with rust water make a green stain.

INGREDIENTS
- Skins from 10-20 onions
- 750ml/1¼ pints White Vinegar (p.24)
- 20ml/4 tsp Rust Water (p.106)

METHOD
Make in the same way as the Grey Wood Stain.

Dark Double Espresso Wood Stain

Used ground coffee works fine for this recipe.

INGREDIENTS

- 1 litre/1¾ pints White Vinegar (p.24)
- 45g/1½oz dried ground coffee

METHOD

Use the vinegar and 22.5g/¾oz of the ground coffee to make an infused coffee vinegar (p.18). To get a stronger stain, make a double infusion, using the first coffee-infused vinegar with the remaining coffee and repeating the process.

Deep Purple Wood Stain

This purple stain can be adjusted to be stronger or deeper depending on how much berry vinegar you add.

INGREDIENTS

- Elderberries
- 750ml/1¼ pints White Vinegar (p.24)

METHOD

Bring the elderberries to boil with a little water. Crush with a potato masher. Leave to stand overnight, then carefully strain and add the vinegar.

Red Wood Stain

Madder root gives an orange to reddish stain, depending on the number of coats. Add a little Rust Water (p.106) for a rich brown.

INGREDIENTS

- 30g/1oz madder root
- 250ml/9fl oz water
- 500ml/18fl oz White Vinegar (p.24)

METHOD

Simmer the madder root and water in a saucepan for 30 minutes, then leave to stand overnight. The next day, add the vinegar and leave to infuse for 1–2 weeks. Strain and use.

Water-based Walnut Wood Stain

Wear gloves when you make this one, as it tends to stain hands. You can stain a lovely golden brown with 1 or 2 coats, or a darker brown with repeated coats.

INGREDIENTS

- 10 walnuts, gathered from the ground, husk on
- 2–4 litres/3½–7 pints water
- White Vinegar (p.24)

METHOD

Add the walnuts and water to a large saucepan, bring to the boil, and continue heating for 12–18 hours, until the liquid is reduced by two-thirds. Remove the walnuts. Add an equal amount of vinegar.

NATURAL PAINT

Modern paints are highly toxic, and often not vegan. Excellent non-toxic, eco-friendly paints are available but expensive, but you can make your own. Plants will provide pigments for homemade paint; I especially like turmeric for yellow and madder for terracotta, both used for centuries as dyes. Plant-based pigments tend to fade. If you want stronger colours that will last longer, use natural mineral earth pigments available online, and put them in with the clay fillers. Any paint is impossible to match completely, so always make enough for a whole job: 2.5 litres/4½ pints will cover 10–12m²/100–130ft sq.

Turmeric Interior Paint

This paint is lovely to work with and makes a natural effect on the wall. You will need to prepare the turmeric-infused linseed oil and turmeric decoction before making this recipe.

INGREDIENTS

- 120g/4oz plain flour
- 500ml/18fl oz cold water
- 750ml/1¼ pints strong turmeric decoction (made with 60–120g/2–4oz turmeric root – fresh if available; p.17)
- Up to a further 1.2 litres/2 pints cold water or turmeric decoction
- 240g/8½oz chalk powder
- 300g/10½oz yellow clay powder
- 80ml/5 tbsp washing-up liquid
- 250ml/9fl oz turmeric-infused linseed oil (p.18)

YOU WILL NEED

- A drill with a paint mixer attachment – this takes a LOT of mixing!

MAKES & KEEPS

Makes about 2.5–3 litres/4½–5¼ pints.
Keeps at least 2 weeks.

METHOD

Add the flour to a large saucepan and slowly add the cold water, mixing well, to make a smooth paste. Add the 750ml/1¼ pints of strong turmeric decoction and heat, stirring briskly, for 2–5 minutes, until you have a thick paste. Remove from the heat, and slowly dilute with up to a further 1.2 litres/ 2 pints of water or turmeric decoction, depending on how strong a yellow you want, whisking all the time.

Add the chalk powder and clay and whisk, then add the washing-up liquid and linseed oil and whisk more until it is the consistency of paint.

Thoroughly mix before each use. To use, apply with a paintbrush. It works best by applying thin coats with 1 hour or more in between coats, and allowing at least 24 hours for the previous coats to dry before applying the final coat.

Terracotta Wall & Wood Paint

This makes a truly lovely brick-red natural paint.

INGREDIENTS

- 120g/4oz plain flour
- 500ml/18fl oz cold water
- 750ml/1¼ pints strong madder decoction (made with 60–120g/2–4oz root)
- Up to a further 1.2 litres/2 pints cold water or turmeric decoction
- 240g/8½oz chalk powder
- 300g/10½oz red clay powder
- 80ml/5 tbsp washing-up liquid
- 250ml/9fl oz madder-infused linseed oil

MAKES & KEEPS

Makes about 2.5–3 litres/4½–5¼ pints.
Keeps at least 2 weeks.

METHOD

Make and use in the same way as the Turmeric Interior Paint (opposite), substituting madder root for turmeric throughout.

Swedish Exterior Paint

COURTESY OF CELTIC SUSTAINABLES

A traditional Swedish recipe for painting exterior wood, said to have a 10 to 15-year lifespan even in the cold and wet Scandinavian climate. This recipe is for a red paint. Ferrous sulphate contains iron that protects against algae growth – if you want a colour other than red, you can use zinc sulphate and another natural earth pigment instead of the red iron oxide pigment.

INGREDIENTS

- 3 litres/5¼ pints water
- 100g/3½oz ferrous sulphate (from garden centres)
- 100g/3½oz finely ground rye flour
- 400g/14oz red iron oxide pigment
- Up to 200ml/7fl oz boiled linseed oil

YOU WILL NEED

- A drill with a paint mixer attachment – this takes a LOT of mixing!

MAKES & KEEPS

Makes approximately 2½ litres/4½ pints of paint.
Make on day of first use, keeps up to 1 week.

METHOD

Bring the water to the boil in a large saucepan and stir in the ferrous sulphate. When it has dissolved, slowly stir in the rye flour and continuously stir while heating the mixture for a further 15 minutes. Next, add the red iron oxide natural earth pigment and continue to stir using the drill with the paint mixer attachment until it is completely mixed in.

Remove from the heat and measure the mixture, then measure out the linseed oil to 8 per cent of the volume – e.g. for every 1 litre/1¾ pints of mixture, add 80ml/5 tbsp of linseed oil. Add the linseed oil to the mixture and stir well to create an emulsion.

To use, mix well. It will dry in 2 hours and usually only needs 1 coat – if doing a second coat, wait 24 hours.

Warm Orange Oil-based Paint

This type of paint works best on wood, bare cement and untreated brick. Marigolds and paprika make a beautiful warm orange when infused with oil. Madder root is a good substitute.

INGREDIENTS

- 750ml/1¼ pints boiled linseed oil
- 30g/1oz dried marigold flowers
- 30g/1oz paprika
- 500ml/18fl oz turpentine
- Peel from 3 oranges
- Orange, yellow or rose natural earth pigment
- Orange oil

MAKES & KEEPS

Makes approximately 750ml/1¼ pints.
Keeps up to 6 months.

METHOD

Use the linseed oil, marigold and paprika to make an infused oil by either hot or cold infusion (p.18). At the same time, make an orange peel-infused turpentine in a sealed jar.

When the infused oil and turpentine are ready, slowly add the infused linseed oil to the natural earth pigment, mixing it to make a putty, then adding more oil until it is pourable. Then add enough of the orange-infused turpentine with some orange oil to thin the paint to the required consistency.

All-natural oil paints take a long time to dry, needing 48 hours between coats. Good preparation is essential. First sand away previous layers of paint and prime the surface with an undercoat of equal parts raw linseed and natural citrus thinner, or a mixture of turpentine and thinner.

Note: turpentine (or turps) is made by distilling pine resin. It is an excellent solvent that is useful in many natural products. It can be used in place of, or along with, citrus essential oil as a thinner for oil paints.

Artists' Oil Paint

The simplest way of making artists' oil paint.

INGREDIENTS

- Linseed or walnut oil
- Your choice of ground plant paint pigments (see box, opposite) or dried clay or earth powder pigments
- Turpentine or citrus oil

MAKES & KEEPS

Makes a variable amount. Make and use fresh.

METHOD

Obtain your pigment from the ground plant, dried clay or earth powder pigments. With a palette knife, gradually mix in a small amount of linseed or walnut oil until you have a thick paste.

You can thin the paint with turpentine or citrus essential oil as needed. Oil paints take 1–3 weeks to dry depending on thickness. Old unused paint can be softened by adding more oil.

Homemade Watercolours

These paints are lovely to work with for adults and children. The colours are strong and beautiful but not permanent.

INGREDIENTS
- 1 tbsp bentonite clay
- 1 tbsp ground plant paint pigment for colour (see box)
- 1 tbsp vegetable glycerine (or water)

MAKES & KEEPS

Makes a variable amount. Keeps 1 week but best made on day of use.

METHOD

Mix together the clay and ground plant paint pigment of your choice. Add a teaspoon of glycerine or water at a time and mix to the desired thickness. If it is too thin, add more clay/plant mix. If it is too thick, add more liquid.

GROUND PLANT PAINT PIGMENTS

Dry the plants then grind to a powder in a coffee grinder or pestle and mortar. Hard materials like roots are best chopped up while fresh then dried.

- Red: beetroot, alkanet or madder root, cranberries, raspberries
- Orange: turmeric, marigold, cayenne pepper, paprika
- Yellow: mustard, pumpkin
- Green: spinach, wheatgrass
- Dark green: spirulina, peppermint, nettle leaves
- Purple: elderberries, bilberry, blueberry
- Brown: coffee, cinnamon, nutmeg, cacao, carob, black walnut
- White: arrowroot or zinc oxide
- Black: soot, activated charcoal

Vegan Tempura-style Paint

Tempura watercolour paint is traditionally made from egg white. This vegan version substitutes flour and cornflour.

INGREDIENTS
- 75g/2½oz cornflour
- 60g/2oz plain flour
- 500ml/18fl oz water
- 1 tbsp washing-up liquid
- Choice of colourings – food colouring or ground plant paint pigments (see box)

MAKES & KEEPS

Makes about five 45ml/3 tbsp pots.
Keeps up to 1 week.

METHOD

In a saucepan off the heat, mix the cornflour and flour with 125ml/4½fl oz water to make a dough. Then put the pan over a low heat and cook, slowly adding a further 250ml/9fl oz of water and whisking for about 10 minutes, until the mixture is totally smooth and getting thick. Take off the heat and whisk in the remaining 125ml/4½fl oz of water. Leave to cool.

Add 1 tbsp washing-up liquid, pour into separate small jars or bowls – one for each colour – and add either the food colourings or ground plant paint pigments. Alternatively, you can use the ground plant paint pigments to make strong infusions and add these in place of the extra water at the last stage of the cooking.

— Tip —

MANY BEAUTIFUL EARTH AND CLAY PIGMENTS CAN BE BOUGHT, OR YOU CAN COLLECT THEM FROM YOUR LOCAL ENVIRONMENT AND MAKE YOUR OWN. BREAK THE MINERALS INTO SMALL PIECES AND COMPLETELY DRY, THEN GRIND TO A POWDER BEFORE USE.

WILD FABRIC DYEING

It is fun and rewarding to use plants as fabric dyes to beautify your home – and for making clothes. Here you will find the simplest way to begin this complex journey.

The following recipes start with food waste, a great free resource for the natural dyer. They then move on to red and blue dyes, indigo and madder, used for thousands of years as dye plants, which you will have to buy or grow for yourself. The first recipe for Golden Onions (p.105) provides the full method. The recipes that follow refer back to it.

First read the preparation instructions below, which apply to any colour dyes.

ALL DYE RECIPES COURTESY OF NATURAL DYER JUSTINE ALDERSEY-WILLIAMS OF THE WILD DYERY IN NORTH-WEST ENGLAND.

— Tip —

WHEN USING WHOLE DYE PLANTS (AS OPPOSED TO GROUND EXTRACTS) YOU'LL NEED 100 PER CENT 'WOF', WHICH MEANS AN EQUAL WEIGHT OF DYE TO FABRIC. HOWEVER, FOR STRONGER SHADES, YOU CAN INCREASE THIS RATIO

YOU WILL NEED
- Very large container/bucket, big enough to loosely submerge the cloth you are dyeing
- Very large saucepan
- Rubber gloves (if you don't want to dye your hands!)

ESSENTIAL PREPARATION

Natural dyes work well on natural fabrics that have been pretreated with an aluminium salt known as a mordant. Mordants create a molecular link between fibre and dye, increasing the longevity of the colour. There are many different mordants, but aluminium acetate is an easy starting point for all types of natural fabric.

All items should first be hot washed (scoured) in an eco-friendly detergent (pp.66-72) to remove coatings and grease, and then dried.

After scouring, weigh your fabric to exactly identify the 'WOF' (weight of fibre). Fill a large container with hot tap water and stir in the mordant aluminium acetate until dissolved. Use 5 per cent by weight, or 5g/just over ⅛oz aluminium acetate for every 100g/3½oz of fabric – for example,10g/⅜oz for 200g/7oz of fabric. Lower the fabric into the solution, move it around to coat evenly and leave until cool. Rinse and dry, ready to use.

Note: different types of fabric, and different mordants used in pretreatment, will tend to affect the finished colour. Be prepared to be surprised!

MAKES & KEEPS

All the following dye recipes, except the Truly Blue Indigo Vat (p.107), make enough for 200g/7oz fabric and the dye is made fresh and used right away. Modify the amounts you need according to your WOF – the weight of the clothes or fabric you are dyeing. The Truly Blue Indigo Vat can be used over and over and keeps for months if properly cared for.

Golden Onions

This gives a lovely golden yellow.
If you add Rust Water (p.106), you'll get green.

INGREDIENTS
- 200g/7oz fabric
- 10g/⅜oz aluminium acetate (mordant)
- 200g/7oz onion skins (red onion creates a slightly different colour)

METHOD
Pretreat the fabric with the aluminium acetate (opposite). Put the onion skins and enough water to submerge your fabric into a large saucepan, bring to the boil and simmer for 30 minutes. Strain the liquid to remove the skins, which could create uneven marks, then return the liquid to the pan and lower the fabric into the dye liquid.

Simmer for 1 hour or until the desired shade is achieved. Fabric dries lighter, so dye it slightly darker than required. For a deep, lasting shade, leave your fabric in the dye solution overnight before rinsing.

Time for Tea

Collect your used black teabags until you have enough to make this lovely beige dye, or add Rust Water (p.106) for a business-like dark grey.

INGREDIENTS
- 200g/7oz fabric
- 10g/⅜oz aluminium acetate (mordant)
- 200g/7oz used teabags

METHOD
Make in the same way as the Golden Onions dye. Remember to scour your clothes (hot wash without fabric conditioner) and dry them before mordanting and dyeing.

Rainbow Rhubarb

This dye can make a few colours, depending on the rhubarb additives. Rhubarb root can dye fabric yellow, orange, green or pink, depending on the species and what you add to it (and perhaps depending on the dyeing angel that day, as natural dyes are never guaranteed to always perform the same!).

INGREDIENTS
- 200g/7oz fabric
- 10g/⅜oz aluminium acetate (mordant)
- 200g/7oz rhubarb root

METHOD
Make in the same way as the Golden Onions dye, but leave the roots soaking overnight after simmering them for 30 minutes. The next day, strain and use the liquid to dye. This will give a yellow-orange colour. If you add Rust Water (p.106) you will get a dark green.

—Tip—

TO ACHIEVE TWO DIFFERENT
SHADES FROM ONE DYE PLANT,
DYE THE FABRIC FIRST, THEN
ADD THE RUST WATER TO THE
DYE BATH AND DIP AREAS OF
YOUR FABRIC INTO IT.

Pink Avocado

It sounds like a contradiction in terms, but in fact avocado skins and stones will dye your fabric a pink-beige. You can also get a beautiful lilac with the addition of rust water.

INGREDIENTS

- 200g/7oz fabric
- 10g/⅜oz aluminium acetate (mordant)
- 200g/7oz avocado skins and stones

METHOD

Make in the same way as the Golden Onions dye (p.105), but leave the skins and stones soaking overnight after simmering them for 30 minutes. The next day, strain and use the liquid to dye. Add a couple of teaspoons of Rust Water for a lilac shade.

Madly Red

Madder root is a red dye plant that will dye fabrics from terracotta to scarlet. You can buy madder extract easily online or buy or grow dried roots. To grow, harvest 3-year-old roots and dry them.

INGREDIENTS

- 200g/7oz fabric
- 10g/⅜oz aluminium acetate (mordant)
- 200g/7oz dried ground madder root or 20g/¾ oz madder extract

METHOD:

Pretreat the fabric with the aluminium acetate (p.104). For dried ground madder root, make in the same way as the Golden Onions dye (p.105). For the extract, prepare it for use by slowly adding warm water to form a paste, then dilute it slowly while stirring to remove any lumps. (The whole root powder method requires straining, the extract method doesn't.)

Rust Water

If you make 'rust water', you can modify the colours created by plant dyes, darkening them. This is known as 'saddening'.

INGREDIENTS

- Handfuls of rusty iron objects – old bed springs, nails, door hinges, etc.
- 250ml/9fl oz White Vinegar (p.24)
- 250ml/9fl oz water

MAKES & KEEPS

Makes 500ml/18fl oz. Keeps indefinitely.

METHOD

Place the rusty objects in a large sealable jar, then add the vinegar and water. Leave for a couple of weeks until the solution begins to change colour. Shake before use, and add a tsp or more of the rust water to a dye bath to modify the colour.

Truly Blue Indigo Vat

Woad and indigo are ancient heritage dyes that have been sacred to people everywhere. Woad is the European dye plant, but indigo produces a stronger colour. For either one, you first make a vat of dye, which can be kept for months and used to dye fabrics over and over. For the recipe, do not use a mordant as a pretreatment.

Note: you can experiment with saddening woad/indigo, but it is less straightforward to work with and you might end up having to restart your vat.

INGREDIENTS

- 25g/1oz natural indigo powder
- 75g/2½oz fructose
- 50g/1¾oz lime (calcium hydroxide)
- 2 tbsp White Vinegar (p.24)

YOU WILL NEED

- 6-7 marbles or pebbles
- Beaker with a lid
- Large lidded bucket (vat)
- pH testing strips

METHOD

Put some marbles or pebbles into a beaker half-filled with warm water, add the indigo powder, put the lid on and shake for 2 minutes. Add the indigo solution to a bucket half-full of warm water. Dissolve the fructose in a little hot water and add to the bucket. Separately, slowly add the lime to warm water, mix to a paste, then add to the bucket. Stir the bucket for 5 minutes, then leave to stand for 24 hours (or 48 for deeper blues). It is ready for use when the dye liquid is a clear yellow and its pH is 10-11. There will be a copper/blue film on the surface of the liquid, which should be moved to the side before dyeing.

To use, put some pottery or stainless steel in the bottom of the vat to stop the fabric touching the sediment, then very gently place damp prewashed fabric into the vat and move it under the surface. Leave it for 10-20 minutes, and squeeze it out as you remove it. Rinse and leave it in the air for 5 minutes, when you will see the fabric change from yellow-green to blue. Repeat the dipping process to get deeper and deeper shades of blue, then finish by rinsing in a bowl of warm water mixed with the white vinegar, followed by a final rinse in water.

The vat can be kept for months, although maintaining your woad/indigo vat in a healthy way is an acquired skill. Keep the lid on. Limit introduction of oxygen by adding wet clothes to the dye and squeezing them as you remove to minimize drips of oxygenated liquid going into the vat, and 'feed' the vat with fructose to reduce oxygen after every use. The alkali pH must also be maintained at around pH 10, so regularly check the pH and add lime to alkalize it to keep it at pH 10–11. Stir vigorously to move all the sediment, then allow to settle for 12–24 hours.

CAUTION

Always wear a face mask when measuring and mixing fine powders.

Wear rubber gloves to handle lime.

Keep ingredients out of reach of children.

VARIOUS ODDITIES

Everything we need comes from plants – including some things we didn't even know existed! From ink to car wax and some weird and wonderful things in between, this section contains a miscellany of useful recipes concocted and gathered over the years.

Zero-waste Vegan Food Wraps

Carnauba wax is a plant-based alternative to the traditional beeswax used for food wraps, but it is much harder and more brittle, therefore less is needed and other ingredients are added to get the right consistency.

INGREDIENTS
- 20g/¾oz pine resin (rosin)
- 15g/4 tsp carnauba wax
- 15ml/1 tbsp olive oil

YOU WILL NEED
- Roughly 50 x 50cm/20 x 20in piece of clean cotton fabric (recycled clothing is fine)
- Greaseproof paper
- Disposable wooden stirring stick
- Paintbrush (reserved for making the wraps)

METHOD
Wash and dry the cotton fabric and cut to the size and shapes you want.

Preheat the oven to 150°C/300°F/Gas Mark 2 and line a baking tray with a double layer of greaseproof paper. Melt together the resin, wax and olive oil in a bain-marie. When the ingredients have melted, continue to heat for a further 5 minutes to ensure they are melded together.

Lay out your first fabric piece on the prepared tray and brush the mixture thinly on to the fabric, working quickly.

Put the tray into the hot oven for a couple of minutes, remove and look to see if any of the cotton seems dry – if it does, brush some more mix on to it. Repeat for the remaining pieces of cotton, placing them over the previously prepared one as you brush on the wax, as that soaks up any excess.

When all the fabric pieces are done, pull them apart and leave them to dry. You can use them in place of clingfilm to wrap cheese, sandwiches, cover tops of pans and so on.

—Tip—

CUTTING THE CLOTH WITH PINKING SHEARS GIVES AN ATTRACTIVE SERRATED EDGE TO YOUR WRAPS.

Waterproofing Mix for Canvas

COURTESY OF TERI EVANS

For waterproofing any type of canvas.

INGREDIENTS
- 250ml/9fl oz soya, grapeseed or almond oil
- 125ml/4½fl oz turpentine

MAKES & KEEPS
Makes 375ml/13fl oz. Keeps at least 1 year.

METHOD
Mix the oil and turpentine together and store in a cool place.

To waterproof, paint 2–3 coats on to dry canvas.

Rose Petal Beads

COURTESY OF KAMALA TODD

The original Rosary prayer beads.

INGREDIENTS
- 2½ litres/4½ pints fragrant, fresh rose petals
- Spring water

YOU WILL NEED
- Iron pot or cauldron

KEEPS
Well-made beads can last over 100 years!

METHOD
Put the rose petals into a little spring water in the iron pot and cover with a lid. Gently simmer (never boil hard as the essential oils will be lost) for 5 hours a day for up to 5 days. Add more water as required to stop the rose petals drying out or burning.

Strain and press the liquid through a muslin cloth to leave a thick, smooth, black paste. Roll the paste into bead shapes using your hands (they shrink to ¼–½ of the size when dry).

Place the beads on a plate and leave in a dry, warm place, away from direct sunlight, for 5–10 days to dry. Roll each day to get a dense, smooth, round bead. Before they are completely dry, push a thick needle or skewer through the middle.

Store fully dried beads in glass jars. Do not allow the beads to get wet.

Gluten-free Playdough

*This playdough can be made plain, or coloured with
food colourings or dried and powdered plant colours.
Make sure the child is not allergic to any of the optional
colours you add.*

INGREDIENTS

- 80g/3oz white rice flour
- 60g/2oz cornflour
- 60g/2oz salt
- 2 tsp lemon juice or cream of tartar
- 250ml/9fl oz water
- 1 tsp coconut oil (or other vegetable oil)
- 1-2 tbsp ground plant paint pigment
  (see box, p.103) (optional)
- 20 drops lemon or orange essential oil
  (optional)

MAKES & KEEPS

Makes approximately 375g/13¼oz.
Keeps up to 3 months.

METHOD

Add all of the ingredients to a saucepan, mix well
and cook over a low heat until it forms a ball.
Remove from the heat and leave to cool completely
before use.

To store, wrap the playdough in Zero-waste
Vegan Food Wraps (p.108) and keep in an
airtight container.

Herbal Mouse Deterrent

*Made from herbs and strong-smelling oils that mice
don't like.*

INGREDIENTS

- 250ml/9fl oz water
- 2 tbsp dried basil
- 2 tbsp dried peppermint
- 2 tsp peppermint essential oil
- 2 tsp rosemary essential oil
- 2 tsp clove essential oil

MAKES & KEEPS

Makes 250ml/9fl oz. Keeps 2 months.

METHOD

Boil the water, then pour it on the herbs and leave to
cool. Strain and add the essential oils to the strong
herb tea liquid. Bottle and store in the fridge.

Shake before use. Soak a cotton wool ball thoroughly
in the strong-smelling mix. Place around the mouse's
entry point to your home. Repeat every 2–4 weeks.

Living Anti-EMF Remedy

There is mounting evidence that radiation from electromagnetic fields can damage our health and mental well-being. You can minimize this by growing houseplants known to absorb the radiation, which we know about thanks to research done by NASA.

INGREDIENTS

Living plants:

- Cactus
- Spider plants
- Ivy
- Aloe Vera
- Asparagus fern

MAKES & KEEPS

Variable

METHOD

Simply obtain and nurture living plants from the list above – one or all of them. Place them all around your home, with key places being by computers, TVs and modems.

Happy Home Charm

ALL SMUDGE STICKS AND CHARMS COURTESY OF
LUCY HARMER

A traditional European charm for a happy home is to place 3 bumblebees that died of natural causes in a pouch with certain herbs. This veganized recipe honours the energy of the bees without making use of their bodies.

INGREDIENTS

- Pinch of dried rue
- 2 oak leaves

YOU WILL NEED

- Felt or paper and coloured paints or pens to make 3 small, happy bumblebees
- A small pouch of natural cloth

MAKES & KEEPS

Makes 1 charm. Keeps 1 year.

METHOD

Make 3 representations of bumblebees, from fabric or drawn and coloured. Put these into a small cloth pouch with the herbs, thinking of your goal. Ask the bees to imbue your pouch with their sweet and happy energy.

Hang the pouch next to the front door.

Sage Cleansing Smoke Stick

Smoke cleansing, which originates in Native American tradition, is a great way to cleanse a space, home or office. Most cleansing smoke sticks are made of sage because it is such a great purifier.

INGREDIENTS
- Several small stalks fresh sage, 15–38cm/6–15in long

YOU WILL NEED
- Thin string or cotton yarn about 1.5m/5ft long

MAKES & KEEPS
Makes 1 stick. Keeps 1–2 years.

METHOD
Lay the sage stalks together so that all the cut ends are facing the same way.

Start winding the string or cotton tightly around the stalks, leaving a 5cm/2in loose end of thread where you began. Wind the string along the length of the bundle until you reach the leafy end.

Return to the stalk end, thus creating a criss-cross pattern. When you get back to the stalks, tie the remainder of the string or cotton to the 5cm/2in loose piece you left at the beginning. Hang the bundle in a dry place for 3–7 days.

When your smudge stick has dried, you can light the leafy end. Allow it to smoulder and send the smoke around a person, an object or your home to cleanse and purify. Snuff the sage out by pressing the stick down on a plate or small bowl – do not extinguish with water as it will be really difficult to light again.

Sage & Lavender Cleansing Smoke Stick

Use to increase mental energy and feel uplifted.

INGREDIENTS
- 5 stalks fresh sage, 15–38cm/6–15in long
- 5 stalks fresh sage, 15–20cm/6–8in long
- 5 stalks fresh lavender, 15–20cm/6–8in long

YOU WILL NEED
- Thin string or cotton yarn about 1.5m/5ft long

MAKES & KEEPS
Makes 1 stick. Keeps 1–2 years.

METHOD
Make in the same way as the Sage Smudge Stick.

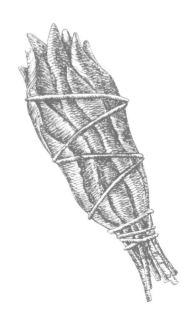

Protection Cleansing Smoke Stick

Use to clear out and cleanse a space of all negative energy and outside influences.

INGREDIENTS
- 3 stalks fresh rosemary, 15–38cm/6–15in long
- 3 stalks fresh lavender, 15–38cm/6–15in long
- 3 stalks fresh juniper, 15–38cm/6–15in long

YOU WILL NEED
- Thin string or cotton yarn about 1.5m/5ft long

MAKES & KEEPS
Makes 1 stick. Keeps 1–2 years.

METHOD
Make in the same way as the Sage Smudge Stick (opposite).

Herbal House-cleansing Stick

An ancient European technique for clearing domestic space.

INGREDIENTS
- 500ml/18fl oz spring water
- 3 large pinches of salt
- 2 sprigs fresh mint
- 2 sprigs fresh rosemary
- 2 sprigs fresh marjoram

MAKES & KEEPS
Makes enough for 1 use. Use immediately.

METHOD
Pour the water into a bowl and add the salt.

Weave the herb sprigs together to make a thick, loose stick.

Dip the stick into the salt water. Sprinkle around the inside and outside of the home.

— Variation —

ADD A LITTLE FRESH
MUGWORT TO THIS BUNDLE FOR
A MORE HEALING VIBRATION.

Good Sleep Charm

INGREDIENTS

- 2 tsp dried mugwort
- 2 tsp dried rue
- 2 tsp dried lavender
- 2 tsp dried angelica
- 2 tsp dried chamomile

YOU WILL NEED

- A small pouch of natural cloth

MAKES & KEEPS

Makes 1 charm. Keeps 1 year.

METHOD

Put the ingredients into the pouch, thinking of your goal.

Squeeze the pouch to release the herbs' fragrance. Hang on a bedpost or place under your pillow for protection while asleep and for good dreams.

House Protection Charm

Many herbs were traditionally known to bestow magical protection.

INGREDIENTS

- 1 tsp dried vervain
- 1 tsp dill seeds
- 1 tsp dried rosemary leaves
- 1 tsp dried bay leaves
- 1 tsp dried St John's wort
- 1 tsp juniper berries
- Pinch of salt

YOU WILL NEED

- A small pouch of natural cloth

MAKES & KEEPS

Makes 1 charm. Keeps 1 year.

METHOD

Put the ingredients into the pouch, thinking of your goal.

Squeeze the pouch to release the herbs' fragrance. Hang next to the front door to bring protection to your home and ward off evil.

Good Luck Charm

*The herbs and crystals in this charm traditionally
bring good fortune.*

INGREDIENTS
- 4 oak leaves
- Small piece of dried heather
- 1 tsp dried orange peel
- 1 acorn
- 1 citrine quartz crystal

YOU WILL NEED
- A small pouch of natural cloth

MAKES & KEEPS
Makes 1 charm. Keeps 1 year.

METHOD
Put the ingredients into the pouch,
thinking of your goal.

Squeeze the pouch to release the herbs' fragrance.
Hang it next to the front door or carry it with you
through the day.

Prosperous House Charm

To call abundance into your home.

INGREDIENTS
- 1 tsp oats
- 1 tsp cloves
- 1 tsp small pieces of cinnamon stick
- 1 tsp mandrake root
- A few gold flakes

YOU WILL NEED
- A small pouch of natural cloth

MAKES & KEEPS
Makes 1 charm. Keeps 1 year.

METHOD
Put the ingredients into the pouch,
thinking of your goal.

Squeeze the pouch to release the herbs' fragrance.
Hang it next to the front door to bring abundance
and wealth to your home.

SACRED WOOD RECIPES

The Celts had a sacred alphabet of trees called the Oghams, one of the oldest forms of writing. Each tree was known to have its own special powers, and people worked with them to call certain qualities into their lives.

Magic Wand

Harry Potter has made wands famous, and you can buy quite expensive replicas, but it is more fun to make your own. Wands can be made of many types of wood. The rowan ogham was 'Luis', considered a magical and protective tree.

INGREDIENTS
- Rowan stick (or other wood), length of your choice

MAKES & KEEPS
Makes 1. Keeps indefinitely.

METHOD
To make a wand, first find a friendly rowan tree (also known as mountain ash) in the spring or summer. If rowans don't grow near you, find a tree that you feel very drawn to. Make an offering to the tree (p.11) and get into a child-like state of non-judgement so you can communicate with the tree, asking its permission to take some of its body for your wand. Once you have a 'yes', you can cut your wand, which should be as long as from your elbow point to your middle finger.

Take the stick home and let it dry for a few days, then strip off the bark and sand it, making the tip into a nicely rounded point.

Use as a toy and who knows what else!

Alder Shield

The alder is a tree that likes to grow near water, and has blood red wood that 'bleeds' red sap when cut. This shield is symbolic, working as a spiritual shield, and can be made quite small. The ogham name is Fearn.

INGREDIENTS
- Fresh alder twigs
- String or twine

MAKES & KEEPS
Makes 1 shield. Keeps 1 year.

METHOD
Sit with an alder tree, make your offering (p.11) and ask its permission to borrow its medicine. When you feel a 'yes', carefully cut twigs from places the tree won't miss them.

Make a circle from one bendy branch and tie it closed. Cross it with two sticks to make a Celtic cross, and tie with twine to keep it firm. Now simply weave as many small twigs and sticks in and out of the frame until it is completely filled.

Yarrow Stalks for I Ching

Yarrow sticks were traditionally used in divination for the I Ching, the ancient Chinese 'Book of Changes'.

INGREDIENTS
- Freshly cut, flowering yarrow stalks

MAKES & KEEPS
Makes 1 set. Keeps indefinitely.

METHOD
Gather your yarrow stalks after making an offering (p.11), cutting from the bottom of the stalks.

Hang the plants up to dry in a dark, warm place for 1 week. Strip the leaves and flowers off of the stalks – do this into a large bowl or on a sheet to collect all the bits. Store the flowers and leaves and use as tea. Take the bare stalks and cut into equal sizes of 15–25cm/6–10in long (depending on the size of your stalks, you may get 1, 2 or 3 from each one). |Use the yarrow stalks as described in the I Ching.

Stinging Nettle String

Stinging nettles make excellent string. Their tough fibres can also be spun into yarn and used to make cloth.

INGREDIENTS
- 10 or more fresh nettle stalks (tall, long, straight ones are needed)

MAKES & KEEPS
Keeps indefinitely.

METHOD
Wearing gloves, pull the nettle out of the ground. Rub the stinging hairs and strip the leaves off the stalk.

Cut about 2.5cm/1in off the bottom and top of the stalk.

Crush the stalk all the way along with your fingers. Put a fingernail in at the base and open it up all the way to the top, spreading it open like a book. Bend the flattened stalk over a finger, with the inside facing upwards, to snap the inside fibres. Carefully peel off and discard these.

The nettle's tough outside fibres can be plaited to make a cord. Take 2 or more fibres together and secure one end. Twist both from the other end, then fold them in half. The 2 twisted sides will twist together and naturally form a strong cord.

Leave the cord to dry somewhere warm for 2 hours.

Chapter Five

HERB DIRECTORY

ACHILLEA MILLEFOLIUM

Yarrow

Long used to staunch wounds (on battlefields and elsewhere), yarrow's pinky white flowers and feathery leaves grace many a field and grassland area in temperate zones across the world.

USES *Yarrow has probably more medicinal uses than any other herb. It is also helpful in the garden because its root secretions are known to be strengthening to other plants, making them more resistant to disease, and the plant repels harmful insects. The stalks have been used since ancient times in China for divination with the I Ching.*

AGRIMONIA SPP.

Agrimony

A 1m/3ft tall perennial herb with carrot-like leaves, agrimony is green on top and silvery underneath, with thin spikes of small yellow flowers. It prefers a wet habitat.

USES *Agrimony is a traditional magical protection herb. It can also be used as a yellow dye, the whole plant harvested from September. The later it is harvested the darker the dye. It has many uses as a medicine.*

AESCULUS HIPPOCASTANUM

Horse Chestnut

This majestic tree, a native of south-eastern Europe, is now cultivated throughout the world. It produces fragrant candles of small flowers and a profusion of brown, shiny, nut-like seeds, protected by spiky green cases.

USES *The seeds or 'conkers' are used in internal and external medicines to strengthen blood vessels, especially the veins. Around the house they are useful due to their saponin content – saponins are soap–like and have detergent properties. Ground conkers are abrasive and useful in scouring mixtures.*

ALLIUM SATIVUM

Garlic

The bulb of this typical, easy-to-grow member of the onion family is used in cooking all over the world. Its cousin, *Allium ursinum* (wild garlic, bear garlic or ramsons) – available online to grow from seeds – grows all over Europe and can be used similarly.

USES *Garlic is highly effective in fighting infections of all kinds. It does this for plants as well as for people, so is a good ingredient in insecticides and antifungal treatments for the garden.*

ANGELICA ARCHANGELICA

Angelica

 A tall and powerful aromatic bitter of the Umbelliferae family, angelica has tiny flowers with distinctive, umbrella-shaped flower heads. Angelica is found most often growing alongside rivers, preferring damp and shady places. Originally native to Syria, it is now widely cultivated.

Take care when collecting this herb as angelica can easily be mistaken for hemlock, which is highly poisonous.

USES *As well as its many uses in herbal medicine, angelica was said to call the angels, so it has many uses in energetic or magical herbalism.*

ARMORACIA RUSTICANA

Horseradish

 Horseradish is a perennial member of the cabbage family native to Europe and western Asia, then introduced to North America though European colonialization. It has strong, large green leaves, small white flowers and a white, tapered root.

USES *Though best known as a culinary herb due to its strong, peppery taste, horseradish root is also an anti-infection medicine. It is a useful ingredient in insecticides for plants.*

ARTEMISIA ABROTANUM

Southernwood

 Another member of the *Artemisia* group like sagebrush, southernwood (also known as 'lad's love' and 'garderobe') is native to Europe, Asia and Africa and now naturalized in parts of the United States. It is a small, bushy shrub with grey-green, narrow feathery leaves, small yellow flowers and a strong camphor-like smell.

USES *Moths do not like it at all so it makes an excellent repellent, which also works for other insects. It is strongly antibacterial and can be used in smudge sticks. A yellow colour can be extracted from the branches, traditionally used for dyeing wool.*

ARTEMISIA TRIDENTATE

Sagebrush

 The *Artemisia* genus is common throughout the world, this particular species being native to the North American West, where it is common throughout. It is an evergreen shrub with tough woody stems and small, pale silver-grey leaves that grows 50cm–3m/ 19½in–9¾ft tall. It has a wonderful aroma.

USES *The wood is highly flammable due to its camphor-like oil content so makes a good firewood. It is a plant traditionally used by the indigenous people of the lands where it grows as a medicine and for smudging – burning the smoke to clear energy (p.112). Recent research has found smudging could clear disease-causing microbes.*

ARTEMISIA VULGARIS

Mugwort

Also known as chrysanthamum weed, mugwort grows over most of Europe and North America. The under leaves are white, the flowers white/green and small, but in profuse spikes.

USES *Mugwort is a medicinal herb that is also burned as an incense. It has many uses in energetic herbalism, being able to move and clear energy – mugwort is used in acupuncture in a procedure called 'moxibustion', where it is burned into the patient's skin. It is protective and is said to help to develop lucid (conscious) dreaming.*

AZADIRACHTA INDICA

Neem

Neem trees, part of the mahogany family, are common in India. They grow to 15–20m/50–65ft or sometimes taller. Neem is evergreen and has leaves made of small leaflets, arranged in pairs opposite each other along a central stem.

USES *A powerful pesticide, neem is used to protect crops from infestation. It yields a strong oil that has many uses in medicine, being antibacterial and antifungal. The oil is widely used in India for soap making.*

CALENDULA OFFICINALIS

Pot Marigold

Originally from southern Europe, pot marigold grows in any temperate climate and is now found all over the world. It is easy to grow and ideal for novice gardeners. The vibrant orange flowers have medicinal uses.

USES *Pot marigold is one of the most versatile and amazing plants. It is legendary as a healing plant, and is strongly antibacterial, antifungal and antiviral, making it an excellent surface cleaner. An infused oil of marigold is a beautiful orange-golden colour, so it is useful also as a wood treatment.*

CALLUNA VULGARIS

Heather

Heather is a tough, low-growing shrub found on moors and heath throughout Europe and Turkey. It likes acid soils. It has small khaki-green leaves and clusters of beautiful flowers which appear in August, white to pink to deep purple-pink.

USES *As well as being used in herbal medicine and to make brooms, heather is traditionally considered to be lucky, so is used whenever good fortune is wanted.*

CAMELLIA SINENSIS

Tea

Camelia sinensis is the source of tea, known all over the world as a refreshing drink. It is a small evergreen tree or shrub native to China. The flowers are a yellowish white with 7–8 petals, the leaves up to 15cm/6in long and 5cm/2in wide, often smaller and lighter when young, ageing to a dark green. It is the leaves that are dried to make tea.

USES *Not only a drink with the reputation, at least in its green state, of being beneficial to health, tea can also make an impressive dye. My favourite is when it is 'saddened' (p.105) to a beautiful grey by adding rusty iron and vinegar.*

CAPSICUM SPP.

Cayenne Pepper

Cayenne is a hot chilli pepper with long green fruits that usually turn red on ripening. It is native to both South and Central America.

USES *Cayenne pepper fruits are much used in herbal medicine. They can be used as an insecticide for plants, and to deter cats from scratching your carpet. They also give up an orange colour, although its relative paprika is a stronger orange. Keep it away from the eyes and wash hands after handling it.*

CANANGA ODORATA

Ylang Ylang

An extremely fast-growing tropical tree native to Indonesia, India and parts of Australia, ylang ylang grows up to 12m/40ft high. It is evergreen with dark green, glossy leaves. The star-shaped greenish flowers are highly fragrant.

USES *Ylang Ylang flowers yield an essential oil with a unique and fun fragrance. It has many medicinal uses including helping hormone balance. It is antibacterial and antiparasitic, and is an excellent insect repellent.*

CEDRUS SPP.

Cedar

There are many trees in the cedar family, coniferous and native to the Himalayas and Mediterranean mountainous regions. They can grow up to 30–40m/100–130ft or even taller and often have reddish scented wood with cracked bark and many thick branches. The leaves are short needles of deep green.

USES *Cedar is repellent to moths and insects. The oil has a pleasant aroma beneficial to wood and with relaxing effects on the mood. It is antifungal and antiseptic as well as insecticidal.*

CERATONIA SILIQUA

Carob

Carob pods come from a beautiful evergreen tree in the pea family. With acacia-like rounded leaves, the pea-like flowers (which smell like human semen!) grow into large, very dark brown seedpods.

USES *The tree has many uses as medicine (the Bedouins use it for sore throats and as a natural Viagra) and food (it makes great desserts, with a taste similar to chocolate). The interior flesh of the pods is dried to make carob powder, which makes a rich dark brown colour for paint and wood stain. The black seeds yield a gum known as locust bean gum, which is used in the food industry as a thickener.*

CHRYSOPOGON ZIZANIOIDES

Vetivert

A tussock grass from India, vetivert is similar to lemongrass, growing up to 3m/10ft tall with long leaves and typically grass-like brownish purple flowers. Vetivert has extremely deep and wide roots, from which an essential oil is distilled.

USES *Vetivert oil has an unusual and powerful odour. Although it is relaxing, it improves brain function and alertness. It has been found to be useful for attention deficit hyperactivity disorder (ADHD) and is used in magic spells and charms. It is a great addition to room sprays.*

CINNAMONUM VERUM

Cinnamon

Cinnamon is a bushy laurel-like evergreen tree from Sri Lanka, Burma and Southern India. The oval leaves are red when young and green when mature. The part used for the familiar spice known throughout the world is the inner bark.

USES *Cinnamon is strongly aromatic and the oil antibacterial like most essential oils. It is widely used in perfumery, food and medicine. The bark itself makes a lovely addition to potpourri and can be infused in oil used for wood treatments. The oil is added to household products for its delicious smell and antibacterial action.*

CITRUS × AURANTIUM

Grapefruit

A citrus tree that is a hybrid of sweet orange and pomelo, originating in Barbados, it is 5–6m/16–20ft high and similar in appearance to orange, lemon and other citrus, but the fruit is a large pale yellow and they grow in grape-like clusters on the tree.

USES *Grapefruit oil is rich in limonene like the other citrus oils and is therefore a useful solvent and cleaner. It has a distinctive fresh, tangy smell, making it a lovely addition to room sprays, laundry liquids, cleaning products and wood treatments.*

CITRUS × LIMON

Lemon

Lemons come from a species of small evergreen tree native to India but now cultivated around the world. The tree grows to 3–6m/10–20ft high. Its twigs usually have sharp thorns and oval leaves that are pointed and shiny. The small flowers have 4–5 petals, white above and purplish beneath; the fruit is so well known it does not need description.

USES *Widely used as a medicine and in cooking, the juice of the lemon is also a preservative. One of the most powerful natural cleaning agents known, it is high in citric acid and a solvent that can lift grime and oily residues and polish wood and other surfaces. It can also be used to thin down and preserve oil paints.*

CITRUS × SINENSIS

Orange

Citrus × sinensis is the sweet orange. Its close cousin is bitter orange, *Citrus × aurantium*. Both are cultivated hybrids of mandarin (*Citrus reticulata*) and pomelo. The trees grow up to 10m/33ft high. The leaves are oval and scalloped, the small flowers fragrant.

USES *Delicious-smelling orange oil from the rind of sweet orange contains a solvent that can be used in household products including wood conditioners and detergents. The peel is a good slug repellent for gardeners. The bitter orange yields neroli and bergamot oils from its flowers, and petigrain from its leaves and twigs.*

COCOS NUCIFERA

Coconut

The coconut tree is a large palm that can grow up to 30m/100ft tall. It is found across the southern part of the world, from Indonesia and South-east Asia through India and Sri Lanka to South America. It produces large fruit with a green outer layer, a brown husky middle shell and a fleshy white inside containing liquid.

USES *It has been vital to the local populations everywhere it grows, having so many uses from construction to medicine and food. The oil can be used as a cleaning and polishing agent as it has antifungal properties and it is also used in soap manufacture. The aroma of coconut is soothing to dogs.*

COFFEA SPP.

Coffee

There are more than 100 *Coffea* species of shrubs or small trees native to tropical and southern Africa and tropical Asia, now grown in Central and South America and the Caribbean as well. *C. arabica* and *C. canephora* are the most used for their seeds, known as coffee beans, to make a drink loved throughout the world. It is one of the most important exports of several countries.

USES *Interestingly, ground coffee can be used for a variety of cleaning purposes, and also gives a rich dark brown pigment to wood stains and paints.*

COPERNICIA PRUNIFERA, C. CERIFERA

Carnauba Wax Palm

This palm tree is native to north-east Brazil. It grows up to 20m/65ft and is 25cm/10in around the trunk. They grow in large numbers on flood plains and around rivers. The small black fruits are food for many animals, the trunk is used in building, and the leaves are a source of a very useful edible wax known as carnauba.

USES *Carnauba wax can be used as a vegan alternative to beeswax. It is a very hard and brittle wax, so to convert beeswax recipes use ½ to ⅔ of the amount of beeswax recommended and add some appropriate vegetable oil such as olive or walnut oil.*

CURCUMA LONGA

Turmeric

This tropical plant is native to South India, and is widely grown in hot and wet areas of the tropics. Its large green leaves grow to around 1m/3ft and its flowers are whitish green. The yellow rhizomes (roots) are used in cooking. Turmeric is considered to be an exceptionally powerful medicinal plant.

USES *A supreme medicine useful in any inflammatory condition, from asthma to arthritis to cancers, turmeric also makes a bold yellow dye. It is antibacterial and antifungal too and repels insects including mosquitos, so using it in wall paints not only gives colour but protection.*

CORIANDRUM SATIVUM

Coriander

A herbaceous annual growing across southern Europe and North Africa and in parts of Asia, this highly aromatic, delicate plant with feathery grows up to 50cm/20in. Its flowers are white or pinkish white, growing in the typical clusters of the Umbelliferae family.

USES *Well known as a delicious and versatile culinary herb, coriander is also medicinally active, and its insecticidal properties make it of use in horticulture.*

CYMBOPOGON SPP.

Lemongrass

This big, bushy, quite tough grass is native to Asia, Africa, Australia and tropical islands. The numerous species make various strongly lemon-scented oils including citronella.

USES *Lemongrass and its various essential oils are antimicrobial, repel insects and are strongly deodorizing, so are a great addition to any cleaning sprays and insect repellents as they protect against ticks. As lemongrass is antibacterial and antifungal, you can also add it to surface cleaners.*

DRACAENA SPP.

Dragon's Blood

Dragon's blood is actually the name of a substance made in ancient times from the resin of various trees of the *Dracaena* genus, among others. Its origins are thought to be from the Canary Islands and Morocco. These thick-trunked, strong-leaved trees tend to grow in arid areas.

USES *The sap that exudes from the tree hardens and dries into a deep red resin that can be used as a medicine as well as an incense, and in varnish production as a dye. It has been thought to have strongly magical properties, especially for protection.*

HAMAMELIS SPP.

Witch Hazel

Witch hazel is a deciduous shrub or very small tree with long, thin oval leaves with a wavy margin. The flowers with four long, thin yellow petals come early, while last year's fruit is still on the tree.

USES *A distilled water is made from the bark, leaves and flowers that is antiseptic and useful as a cleaning product and as a carrier for added oils.*

EUCALYPTUS GLOBULUS

Eucalyptus

This elegant tree of the myrtle family, native to Australia, can grow to 45m/148ft. It has smooth, pale-coloured bark and long, dark green shiny leaves full of a highly aromatic and flammable oil.

USES *Eucalyptus oil has a distinctive odour, being cleansing for the nose and sinuses and helpful to the lungs. Like most essential oils, it is antibacterial and antiviral, making it a useful addition to multi-surface cleaners and air fresheners for use around the home. It is also a very effective insect repellent.*

HEDERA HELIX

Ivy

The common ivy is a climbing plant with distinctive bright green or variegated dark and light leaves. Some parts of the plant have simple oval leaves, some a longer pointed middle part and two smaller scalloped sides. Ivy is commonly found climbing up walls and trees. It has small greenish-yellow aromatic flowers and small round fruits.

USES *Not to be confused with the US and Asian poison ivy, which looks totally different and is not in the same family, common (English) ivy is rich in saponins and can be used as a simple soap.*

HELIANTHUS ANNUUS

Sunflower

 Belonging to the daisy family, this beautiful annual has a strong, thick stem and grows up to 4m/13ft tall. The domestic species produces one very large flower head with a brownish centre and large, warm yellow petals. Like other daisy family members, the head is made of many tiny flowers, and the centre of each of these may mature to a seed.

USES *Sunflower seeds are edible and yield a rich oil widely used in cooking, medicine and as an ingredient in vegetable soaps. The flowers grace potpourri and dried arrangements, and it is a happy plant to grow in the garden both for people and pets to enjoy.*

HYPERICUM PERFORATUM

St John's Wort

 This beautiful wayside weed with small yellow flowers is indigenous to Europe, but introduced in temperate zones of the Americas. If you hold the leaves up to the light, you will find little see-through dots: these are oil glands.

USES *Famous in herbal medicine for many reasons, the infused oil is a lovely red colour and so a useful ingredient in polishes, leather and wood treatments.*

ISATIS TINCTORIAL

Woad

 Dyer's woad is a cabbage-family flowering plant native to Russia and parts of Asia but now found in Europe and North America. Large, abundant green leaves and yellow flowers similar to others of its family, woad grows up to about 1m/3ft tall.

USES *Woad has been used since ancient times to create a blue dye. To do this, it must be treated in a certain way. The dye is called 'woad indigo' and is similar (although weaker) to that obtained from the non-European indigo plant,.*

JUGLANS NIGRA

Black Walnut

 This beautiful tree is native to the USA but has been widely introduced in Europe. It produces a fruit that falls with its husk, green, in the autumn, and this green fruit, along with the leaves and flowers, all have many uses.

USES *Walnut hulls make a brownish-black dye, while the flower makes a remedy to help adjust to periods of change. The oil is a hardening oil so useful as a polish and wood treatment.*

JUNIPERUS COMMUNIS

Juniper

Common juniper is widespread throughout Europe and the East. A robust shrub that likes cooler climes or higher altitudes in more southern locations, this evergreen has many small, needle-like leaves, each with one white bank. It makes small, aromatic, nearly black berries.

USES *Juniper has many medicinal uses – as a cleansing, antiseptic aromatic plant to burn and as an oil. It is antiviral as well as antifungal and antibacterial. It is traditionally used in protection and cleansing.*

LARIX SPP.

Larch

A rarity in the conifer group in that it is deciduous (it loses its leaves in autumn), the graceful larch is found throughout the cooler climes of the temperate north. It grows 20–60m/65–200ft tall and has delicate, light green, needle-like leaves.

USES *Oil from larch is a moth repellent and very strongly antibacterial. It can be used in any recipe in place of pine.*

LAVANDULA ANGUSTIFOLIA AND SPP.

Lavender

This aromatic, purple-flowered perennial prefers dry, well-drained soils and lots of sun. It is grown commercially mainly for production of its essential oil, which is antiseptic and anti-inflammatory. Many related species have similar properties. It has been cultivated across Europe, Asia and Africa for thousands of years.

USES *Lavender is widely used in cooking and medicine. The oil it is rich in is antiseptic and with its unique smell it is a great addition to cleaners, air fresheners, potpourris and many household products.*

LINUM USITATISSIMUM

Common flax

Also known as linseed, flax is a crop cultivated in temperate zones. It grows around 1m/3ft tall with slender pointed leaves and pale blue, five-petalled flowers. It produces a round fruit that contains several small, brown, shiny seeds.

USES *Linen is woven from flax stalks, and the seeds yield linseed oil, which is used as an excellent source of the important omega-3 essential fatty acids needed for health of the heart, brain and joints. It is also a mainstay of care for wood, being the key ingredient in polishes, cleaners, preservatives and oil paints. Linseed is a rare 'drying oil', which means it turns into a solid form when applied to surfaces and does not then go rancid.*

MALUS SPP.

Apple

Apple is a deciduous tree growing up to 9m/30ft tall in the wild, though half the height in cultivation. The blossom is pink-white and fragrant, the familiar fruits round, covered in a green, yellow or red waxy skin with juicy flesh within. *M. domestica* is the most commonly cultivated species, though this is often mixed in some way with the crab apple, *M.sylvestris*. Apples grow in many cooler parts of Europe, Asia and China and are also cultivated in the USA.

USES *As well as food and medicine, apples can be made into alcohol and vinegar, which is made from the skins and cores of apples and then used as a cleaning product and preservative for other plants.*

MATRICARIA CHAMOMILLA

Chamomile

A much-loved member of the daisy family with small yellow and white flowers and a distinctive fragrance. It is native to Europe and Asia. A close relative, *Anthemis nobile*, or Roman chamomile, is similarly used.

USES *It has many uses in the home having soothing and gentle antiseptic with anti-inflammatory properties. In herbal medicine it is known as 'the mother of the gut' and is enormously useful.*

MELALEUCA ALTERNIFOLIA

Tea Tree

A very commonly grown Australian tree or shrub related to myrtle, tea tree grows up to 7m/23ft tall. It has thin, light-coloured bark and a thick crown. The pale green leaves are long and thin, rich in a strong-smelling oil.

USES *Tea tree oil is a magnificent antiseptic and antifungal substance so finds many uses around the home.*

MELISSA OFFICINALIS

Lemon Balm

This sweetly lemon-scented hardy perennial is naturalized all over the UK and USA. Similar to mint in appearance, but with bright green leaves and small whitish flowers, it has also been known as 'heart's delight'.

USES *Lemon balm is a much-loved medicinal herb with many applications. It is a wonderful addition to air fresheners and room sprays, having a powerful uplifting effect and dissolving anxiety.*

MENTHA PIPERITA AND SPP.

Peppermint

Peppermint is a herbaceous perennial with square stalks and opposite dark green pointy leaves, growing 30–90cm/12–35in. It is very easy to cultivate, spreading by underground roots to form new plants. Mints tend to prefer damp and shady habitats, and are easily recognizable by their distinctive smell and taste.

USES *Rich in an essential oil that gives it many of its properties, mint has numerous medicinal uses. Dogs love it, mice hate it, it gives a green colouration when infused in linseed oil or used as paint, and its fresh, stimulating smell is used in cleaning products, car screen wash, polish, potpourri, air fresheners, you name it.*

MYRISTICA FAGRENS

Nutmeg

The fragrant spice known as nutmeg comes from the fruit of an evergreen green tree with dark green leaves that can grow in some cases up to 30m/100ft tall. It is native to the spice islands of Indonesia and is cultivated in the West Indies.

USES *Nutmeg is highly aromatic, antibacterial and can be used for its fragrance and its germ-busting properties in the home. It is a powerful insect repellent and can also be used as a stomach medicine.*

NICOTIANA TABACUM

Tobacco

Tobacco is a strong annual herbaceous plant growing up to 2.5m/8¼ft tall with large sticky green leaves and long trumpet-shaped pinkish white flowers. The sticky secretion it covers itself with contains the highly toxic nicotine.

USES *Tobacco is a very poisonous plant and therefore an excellent insecticide, useful especially for infestations of home and garden plants.*

OCIMUM BASILICUM

Basil

Basil is a strongly aromatic member of the mint family, with shiny green leaves and very small white flowers. Native to India, it has been cultivated in southern Europe and across Asia for thousands of years. It is easy to grow on a sunny windowsill.

USES *Basil, a well-known culinary herb, is a powerfully antiviral and antimicrobial plant, and is a valuable ally in cleaning. Its beautiful scent and relaxing effect make it perfect for home fragrances. It is also said to bring abundance and happiness.*

OLEA EUROPAEA

Olive

The olive is a small tree found throughout the Mediterranean, Levant, Arabia and China. It is a small evergreen tree growing up to 15m/50ft, with small silver green leaves and a gnarled grey trunk. It makes a small fruit from which olive oil is extracted.

USES *Olive oil, as well as being a health-giving food, has many uses around the home. It can be used as a polish and cleaning agent, and is great for making infused plant oils or as a carrier for essential oils.*

ORIGANUM VULGARE

Oregano

Oregano and its close cousin, *O. marjorana* (marjoram), are native to the Mediterranean and Asia. Both are small-leaved, highly aromatic members of the mint family, with tiny, pink-purple flowers. They prefer the heat and a well-drained soil, but can be surprisingly hardy when grown.

USES *Oregano and marjoram are well-known culinary herbs that lend a distinctive 'Italian' flavour to dishes. Both are antiseptic, antiviral and bactericidal so are useful for home cleaning. They are very much used in herbal medicine.*

PELARGONIUM GRAVEOLENS

Geranium

This geranium of the large geranium family is the source of the essential oils geranium and rose geranium. The lobed and notched leaves of this now widely cultivated South African native are aromatic and pale green and the small yet beautiful flowers a pale pinkish red. The houseplant 'lemon geranium' is a close relative.

USES *Geranium oil is emotionally uplifting as well as being antifungal, antiviral and antibacterial – it is very active against Staphylococcus aureus and is one of the oils that may be of benefit against MRSA. It is a useful ingredient in household products as it has energetically protective effects, being stress-reducing, and aiding sleep and relaxation.*

PINUS SPP.

Pine

There are more than 100 conifers known as pines, evergreen resinous trees growing 3–80m/10–260ft tall, some living up to 1,000 years. They like cooler climes, being found only in the northern hemisphere in Europe, North America, South-east Asia and Russia.

USES *Many types of pine have uses in the home in addition to their powerful medicinal actions. Pine is antibacterial and antifungal, making it an antiseptic addition to cleaners of all kinds. The resin of pine has many uses, from its raw state in vegan re-use waxed food wraps to the turpentine that is made from it, in paints and wood treatments.*

Pomegranate

The delicious fruit known as pomegranate comes from a shrub or small tree originating in Mesopotamia (Iran). It has spiny branches with opposite leaves and bright yellow to red flowers and grows up to 10m/33ft high but usually smaller.

USES *Cultivated throughout the Middle East and the Mediterranean as well as parts of India and Africa, it is also found in the South-western USA. Not only is it lovely to eat with health-giving properties, but it is useful as a source of natural yellow to pink-orange fabric dye. Its beauty and energy of abundance makes it a lovely potpourri ingredient to decorate a house.*

QUERCUS SPP.

Oak

Oak is a long-living, tall-growing tree found throughout the northern hemisphere. It has green spirally arranged leaves, mostly with deeply scalloped edges, and produces a tannin-rich nut called an acorn in great abundance in the autumn that provides food for many.

USES *The oak is home to hundreds of species of insects, animals and birds. It is a symbol of strength, courage and life and said to bring these properties to us. The acorns and galls – small round growths formed on the branches by insects – are tannin-rich and can be used to make a nearly black ink.*

RHEUM SPP.

Rhubarb

Rhubarb is commonly cultivated as a garden plant and its ruby pink stems eaten when well cooked and sweetened. Its leaves are often a rich dark green, large and fleshy, each emanating from its own thick, pink-red stalk.

USES *The roots are yellowish and are used in herbal medicine, as well as producing lovely shades of yellow and orange fabric dyes, or dark green when 'saddened' with rust water (p.106).*

ROSA SPP.

Rose

There are more than a hundred species of roses found all around the world. The species of rose advisable to use for medicine or food include *R. canina, R. arkansa, R. laevigata, R. gallica var. centifolia* and *R. rugosa.*

USES *The flowers and fruits are edible and medicinal along with the oil of the seeds. One of the most beautiful aromas of any plant oil, rose is a luxurious addition to room sprays, potpourris and laundry liquids. The oil is very expensive because it is found in miniscule quantities within the petals – however, it can be used sparingly as it is so strongly aromatic.*

ROSMARINUS OFFICINALIS

Rosemary

This aromatic, perennial, woody-stemmed shrub is native to the Mediterranean and needs plenty of sunlight to flourish fully. Its green-white, needle-like leaves and purple/pink/white or blue flowers smell strongly of the essential oil in which rosemary is rich.

USES *Both the fresh and dried herb and the essential oil are often used in medicines, foods and household products as a good antibacterial. It is traditionally protective against negative energy and is proven to reduce damage from radiation.*

RUTA GRAVEOLENS

Rue

Rue, native to southern Europe, is a small perennial herbaceous shrub with a strong smell. A very ornamental plant for the garden, it has many small, roundish, delicate leaves and tiny yellow-green flowers.

USES *It is used in herbal medicine, and also as an insecticide and cat repellent. It was popular in traditional European magic with many uses from attracting love and money to powerful protection.*

Warning: fresh rue on the skin combined with being in the sun can lead to a blistering dermatitis, so handle the fresh plant with care.

RUBUS TINCTORIUM

Madder Root

Madder is a herbaceous perennial from the same family as bedstraw and coffee. It climbs up to 1.5m/5ft high with small green leaves in whorls around the stem and small hooks on the stem. Tiny pale yellow flowers grow in clusters and mature into small dark red or black berries. The roots can grow over 1m/3ft long and are thick and red.

USES *Madder root is used in herbal medicine, but is most famous as a dye plant, being a source of a true red dye, which is rare in the plant world.*

SALVIA OFFICINALIS AND SPP.

Common Sage

An aromatic flowering herb in the mint family, common sage has grey-green leaves and lilac flowers. It is a Mediterranean native, but is now widely naturalized.

USES *Sage is a culinary herb, delicious in savoury dishes and salads, and is used all around the world as a medicine. It has a particularly deodorizing effect so is useful in air fresheners, and is energetically clearing and protective. The dried herb is burned to clear space of negative energy and germs.*

SAMBUCUS SPP.

Elder

Sambucus nigra in Europe and *S. canadensis* in the USA is a small tree or large shrub. Common in the UK, Europe and North America, it produces creamy white clusters of small flowers that develop into small, juicy, purple-black berries.

USES *Both the berries and flowers of elder are much used in herbal medicine. The berries make a great purple stain and dye.*

SAPONARIA OFFICINALIS

Soapwort

Members of the soapwort family are found all over Europe and Asia. Smallish herbaceous plants with five-petalled pink or white flowers, some species are annuals and some perennials.

USES *S. officinalis, native to Eurasis but now introduced all over the world, can be used to make a liquid soap because it is so full of saponins.*

SAPINDUS SPP.

Soap Nut

Sapindus is a group of small trees and shrubs related to lychees, native to India, Nepal and China. It grows wild in poor soil, the trees growing 9–18m/30–60ft tall. They live for around 100 years, starting to bear fruit in their ninth year. The creamy white flowers grow in a showy bundle and make round yellow berries that ripen into a deep tan, being full of saponins.

USES *The berries are so full of saponins that they can be used for any recipes that require a soapy action.*

SYMPHYTUM OFFICINALE

Comfrey

Comfrey thrives in damp and cool conditions. It has fleshy, dark green, hairy leaves and blue-purple, or sometimes white-pink, flowers. Its black roots conceal a white, gloopy (mucilaginous) interior.

USES *Also known as knitbone, comfrey is famous for healing bone and connective tissue and has many medicinal uses. It makes an excellent food to nourish other plants and gives a rich dark green infused oil for wood treatments and paints.*

SYZYGIUM AROMATICUM

Clove

What we know as the spice 'cloves' are the unopened flower buds of an evergreen tree of the myrtle family. The many-branched tree has smooth oval leaves and very aromatic flowers. Native to Indonesia, the trees grow 8–12m/ 25–40ft. The dark red flowers grow in clusters.

USES *Repellent to moths, ants and other insects, clove is also extremely antimicrobial so can be used in household disinfectants. It is used in magic for protection and healing, and has many medicinal uses including as a pain reliever for toothache, and as a treatment for parasites.*

THYMUS SPP.

Thyme

There are many species of this small-leaved, aromatic herb with woody stems and tiny pink flowers. *Thymus serpyllum*, or wild thyme, is native to southern Europe and a cultivated variety of this, *T. vulgaris*, is grown all around the world.

USES *Thyme contains an essential oil high in 'thymol', a very potent antiseptic that can be used to treat infections including gum disease and cuts and scrapes. As well as its impressive use as a medicine, thyme's antiseptic properties find many applications in home and garden.*

TRITICUM AESTIVUM

Wheat

Wheat is a grass grown as a food crop throughout the world. Its seed is a cereal grain that is rich in carbohydrates and some protein.

USES *Wheatgrass is loved by cats and is full of healthful nutrients. (Wheatgrass shots or wheatgrass smoothies are so nutritious they are said to be able to make grey hair grow coloured again!) The flour is a very versatile substance that is an important ingredient of eco-friendly paints.*

URTICA DIOICA

Stinging Nettle

This perennial plant can grow more than 1m/3ft tall from its network of thin, whitish roots, and has green, sharply serrated leaves. The undersides of the leaves are covered in fine, histamine-containing hairs which sting you if touched. It is native to Europe, USA, Asia and North Africa.

USES *Nettles are one of the great panaceas of the plant world. Rich in minerals, vitamins and amino acids, they are one of the best, and easiest to find, wild plants to use as a food. They have many medicinal applications, and the fibre-rich stalks can be used to make string and cloth.*

VALERIANA OFFICINALIS

Valerian

This strongly smelling, elegant, tall perennial herb is native to Europe and Asia. It has fresh green divided leaves and heads of small pink or white flowers and can grow up to 1.5m/5ft. Note that the common wall-growing plant known as red valerian is actually a completely different plant with the botanical name *Centranthus ruber*, and is not similarly used.

USES *A very important plant in herbal medicine as a relaxant, valerian also finds creative uses in the happy home. Although humans either love or hate the strong smell, cats adore it and dogs are calmed by it. It makes a lovely aromatic water.*

VERBENA OFFICINALIS

Vervain

Common vervain is a European perennial herb growing up to 70cm/28in high. Its delicate, thin-branched stalks grow upright with small-toothed leaves and purple flowers that grow in clusters.

USES *Much used in herbal medicine as a nerve tonic, vervain varieties have been considered sacred to every culture where they grow, from the Celts and Norse folk to the Egyptians. It is a supremely protective plant, illustrated by its many local names, which liken it to iron.*

VANILLA SPP.

Vanilla

Vanilla is a vine of the orchid family. The most common vanilla flavouring comes from the Mexican *V. planifolia* (meaning flat-leaved). The delicate greenish-yellow flowers form a banana-like pod or bean. These are fermented and dried to yield black pods with the distinctive flavour and odour of vanilla, now known throughout the world. The sap of the living plant can cause severe skin irritation.

USES *Vanilla is a fabulous flavouring for food and if you like the smell you can use it in any household product to make you happy. Dogs adore it and it is proven to make them calm and reduce anxiety.*

ZINGIBER OFFICINALE

Ginger

Ginger is an upright herbaceous perennial originating in South-east Asia with many reed-like stalks and long leaves shooting up from an edible rhizome (an underground stem). The plant has cone-shaped pale yellow flowers and grows 60–120cm/2–4ft high.

USES *The rhizomes, which have a pale brown fibrous skin and a yellow, juicy and fibrous interior with a very pungent odour, have many uses. As well as being a medicine and food, ginger is relaxing for dogs and the oil is a strong antibacterial.*

CONTRIBUTORS

I offer grateful thanks to the following plant experts who have kindly shared their recipes.

Justine Aldersey-Williams is a textile designer and teacher specialising in natural fabric dyeing. She runs The Wild Dyery studio in North West England where she teaches live and online training courses.

Celtic Sustainables is a company run by Ian Bowler in Cardigan in Wales that specializes in ecological and sustainable building solutions of all kinds. You can buy coloured earth pigments from them – non-toxic, earth and mineral based pigments.

Teri Evans is a medical herbalist and runs Cunnynge Herbs in Shropshire. Here she sells artisan herbal tinctures and holds workshops on using herbs.

Lucy Harmer is an international author and teacher based in Geneva, Switzerland. She is also a feng shui and space clearing expert, and a high priestess on the Celtic Shamanic Path.

Marc Luyckx is a domestic alchemist in Switzerland.

Joe Nasr is a medical herbalist, osteopath and senior lecturer in herbal medicine, as well as a dedicated and experienced plant distiller. In 1997 Joe founded Avicenna, a company producing unique, high-quality herbal products in Wales.

Tanya Smart runs the Yemoya company in Glastonbury in Somerset, which makes the best organic soaps ever.

Kamala Todd is an artist based in Malvern who makes rose petal bead jewellery.

Michael Vertolli is a Western traditional herbalist who lives in Ontario, Canada. He is the founder and director of the Living Earth School of Herbalism.

Lucy Wells is a plant spirit medicine healer and teacher, a Tai Chi teacher and an artist and writer in Shropshire, UK.

SOURCES & FURTHER READING

Books

Bond, Annie B., 2005. *Home Enlightenment* (Kindle edition)

Booth, Abigail, 2017. *The Wild Dyer: A guide to natural dyes & the art of patchwork & stitch* (Kyle Books)

Jeffery, Josie, 2011. *Seedbombs – Going Wild With Flowers* (Lewes: Leaping Hare Press)

Mabey, Richard, 2012. *Food for Free* (Collins UK)

McIntyre, Anne, 2011. *Drugs in Pots* (London: Gaia)

Michael, Pamela, 1986. *A Country Harvest* (London: Peerage Books)

Neddo, Nick, 2015. *The Organic Artist* (MA: Quarry Books)

Richardson, Anna et al, 2019. *The Children's Forest* (Crafts and Family Activities; UK: Hawthorn Press)

Rose, Lisa M., 2015. *Midwest Foraging: 115 Wild and Flavorful Edibles from Burdock to Wild Peach* (Regional Foraging Series; Timber Press)

Waller, Pip, 2015. *The Herbal Handbook for Home & Health* (NAB)

Waller, Pip, 2018. *The Health & Beauty Botanical Handbook* (Lewes: Leaping Hare Press)

Websites

www.pipwaller.co.uk
(my professional website)

www.touchedbynaturepsm.uk
(for plant workshops with Pip Waller in UK)

www.americanherbalistsguild.com
(for finding a herbalist in the USA)

www.associationofmasterherbalists.co.uk
(for finding a herbalist in the UK)

https://www.celticsustainables.co.uk/

www.ediblewildfood.com
(for great foraging information and recipes)

www.gaianstudies.org
(for USA-based training from
The Foundation for Gaian Studies)

www.globalhealingcenter.com
(for information about growing plants
in the USA)

www.herbnet.com
(for everything herbal in the USA)

www.herbworld.com
(for an online encyclopedia with herbal information)

www.naturalearthpaint.com
(mineral pigments USA/Europe)

www.nimh.org.uk
(the National Institute of Medical Herbalists:
for finding a UK herbalist and herbalist training)

www.thewilddyery.com
(for online and in person courses in
using natural plant dyes)

INDEX

ACKNOWLEDGEMENTS

I would like to thank the many people who have made this book possible. A huge thank you to all at Leaping Hare, particularly the lovely Monica Perdoni, who spotted me during my two-minute *Countryfile* appearance and had the idea, as well as editors Tom Kitch and Charlotte Frost. Also thanks to the designer, Wayne Blades, for making a beautiful book.

Thanks as ever to my parents, Sheila and David Waller, who got me into herbal medicine in the first place by their example, and for all their help and support over the years, and to my mother Kate who gave me life. Thanks also to my friends who tried a lot of weird and wonderful recipes – some that made it, some that didn't – and listened to a lot of gnashing of teeth as I wrestled with the computer over this project.

Thanks to the fabulous herbalists, plant spirit medicine practitioners and plant lovers who generously gave their recipes – you have made this book the interesting and varied mixture of recipes that it is. Thanks to my friends in the plant world, the herbs themselves, for calling to me again and again and waving to me wherever I go. And last but not least, thank you to the One who is behind everything.

The publisher would like to thank the following for the permission to reproduce copyright material.

All photographs are from Shutterstock © Morphart Creation p.9, 15, 19, 28, 32, 46, 49, 52 A, 68, 86 above, 95, 105, 110, 116, 121 below right, 122 below right, 124 above right, 125 below left, 127, 128 above right, 129, 131, 132 above, 133 above, 134, 135 above right, 136 above left; Olga Korneeva 11 above, 33, 35, 42, 45, 48, 54, 58, 75 below; Nadezhda Molkentin 76, 81, 91, 109, 113; JimmyIurii 11 below 30; Slonomysh 31; Hein Nouwens 36, 40, 72, 123 above left, 125 above right, 126 above left, 132 below right; Yevheniia Lytvynovych 43; Jka 47, 51, 97, 101, 111; Doremi 55, 56, 63 below, 82 above, 93; Channarong Pherngjanda 64, 90 below, 100, 125 above left, 128 above left, 130 above left, 137 below left; Mart 67, 94, 99, 102; Komleva 74, 92, 123 below left; Bodor Tivadar 96 below; Adehoidar 106; Babich Alexander 108 below; Lynea 108 above; Monkographic 112; Bubnova Natalia 117; Foxyliam 121 above right; Aniok 122 below left, 135 below left; SThom 123 above right; Graphuvarov 123 below right; Helena-art 124 above left; KosOlga 124 lower left; Right oxygen_8 125 below; NataLima 126 below left; Epine 126 below right; Olena Go 127 above left; Victoria Novak 130 above right; BTSK 133 below left; Alexander_P 136 above right.

All reasonable efforts have been made to trace copyright holders and to obtain their permission for the use of copyright material. The publisher apologizes for any errors or omissions in the list above and will gratefully incorporate any corrections in future reprints if notified.